Hezekiah Butterworth, Lauriat Estes &, Charles Laplante, Theodor Ettling, Paul Philippoteaux

Zigzag journeys in the Occident

the Atlantic to the Pacific

Hezekiah Butterworth, Lauriat Estes &, Charles Laplante, Theodor Ettling, Paul Philippoteaux

Zigzag Journeys in the Occident
the Atlantic to the Pacific

ISBN/EAN: 9783744744546

Printed in Europe, USA, Canada, Australia, Japan

Cover: Foto ©Andreas Hilbeck / pixelio.de

More available books at **www.hansebooks.com**

HOLY CROSS MOUNTAIN.

ZIGZAG JOURNEYS

IN

THE OCCIDENT.

THE ATLANTIC TO THE PACIFIC.

A SUMMER TRIP OF THE ZIGZAG CLUB FROM BOSTON TO THE GOLDEN GATE.

BY

HEZEKIAH BUTTERWORTH,
AUTHOR OF
"ZIGZAG JOURNEYS IN THE ORIENT," "ZIGZAG JOURNEYS IN CLASSIC LANDS," "ZIGZAG JOURNEYS IN EUROPE,"
"YOUNG FOLKS' HISTORY OF AMERICA," "YOUNG FOLKS' HISTORY OF BOSTON."

FULLY ILLUSTRATED.

BOSTON:
ESTES AND LAURIAT,
301-305 WASHINGTON STREET.
1883.

Copyright, 1882,
BY ESTES AND LAURIAT.

All Rights Reserved.

PREFACE.

OMESTEADING!
It is an American word, but one of wonderful meaning. It expresses the early history of those great empires, called States, now forming in the West.

It was the aim of "ZIGZAG JOURNEYS IN EUROPE" to interest the reader in the associations of historic places, and to stimulate historic reading; of "ZIGZAG JOURNEYS IN CLASSIC LANDS," to make attractive classical studies; of "ZIGZAG JOURNEYS IN THE OCCIDENT," to clearly explain the Eastern Question.

It is the purpose of this story-telling volume to explain HOMESTEADING, and to give a glance at the resources of the great Northwest and its opportunities for the emigrant.

A great tide of emigration is pouring into the West, especially the Northwest, from Europe. Young men in the Eastern States are seeking the West in greater numbers than ever before; and families from the Middle States, once called the West, are steadily crossing the Mississippi. This volume, though in the main a book of stories, seeks to show the aim and possible results of the great emigration; what the government's lands are, and how they may be obtained; the conditions of success of the Western homesteader, and the possible profits of his enterprise.

Stories and pictures are profusely used, after the manner of the other Zigzag books. While these methods are open to criticism, they have not proved unpopular, as the Zigzag series of books have already reached a sale of nearly 100,000 volumes.

The previous volumes of the Zigzag books have been considerably used in schools for collateral readings. As the subject of this is associated with one of the most promising and healthful features of American life and history, it is hoped that it may also be found useful for the same purpose.

The author is indebted for helps to Miss ISABELLA T. HOPKINS ("Jerry Slack's Money-Pot"); Mrs. THEODORA R. JENNESS, of Kansas, author of "The Young Homesteaders," ("How John Wyman obtained his One Hundred and Sixty Acres of Land"); JEFF. L. HARBOUR, late editor of a Leadville, Colorado, paper, and several Western pioneers and writers on Western life and enterprises.

H. B.

CONTENTS.

CHAPTER		PAGE
I.	A DISCOVERY	15
II.	A NEW JOURNEY PLANNED	44
III.	CHARLIE LELAND AND GENTLEMAN JO	60
IV.	A MEETING OF THE ZIGZAG CLUB	84
V.	A STORY-TELLING JOURNEY	109
VI.	THE STORY OF DETROIT	142
VII.	THE STORY OF CHICAGO	161
VIII.	ST. PAUL	181
IX.	MINNEAPOLIS	197
X.	DAKOTA	214
XI.	WONDER-LAND	233
XII.	THE STORY OF MORMONISM	255
XIII.	SAN FRANCISCO	281
XIV.	ANCIENT AMERICA	301

ILLUSTRATIONS.

	PAGE		PAGE
Holy Cross Mountain . . . *Frontispiece.*		Crossing the Mountains	85
Grand Cañon of the Colorado	14	Members of the Zigzag Club	88
A Dakota Town and Farm	16	Young Garfield at the Carpenter's Bench	89
Sweet William	19	Henry Wilson	90
Heroes of the Plains	23	On the Prairie	91
In Search of a Homestead	25	John Wyman crossing the Prairie . .	92
A Settler's Home in the Mountains . .	26	A Western Forest Home	94
A Timber Claim	28	A Prairie Schooner	96
Stock-Raising in the Southwest . . .	29	Rounding up a Herd	100
Gentleman Jo and the Club	33	The Herder's Home	101
"A Message for *me!*"	36	Dalrymple Farm	103
The Message	39	Fargo, Dakota Territory	105
Jerry finds the Money-Pot	42	State House, Boston	110
Horseshoe Cañon	45	Statue of Edward Everett	111
Trees of the Yosemite	47	The Ossipee Stage	112
Giant Geyser	48	The People generally remembered the	
Aborigines	50	Parson	114
Hoodoos	51	"Here, Parson"	116
Mud Volcano	53	He shut his Eyes and threw the Pullet	
Seeding on the Prairie	54	away	118
Scipio's Flight from the Bear	58	He examined it carefully	120
Indian Burial Place	61	Chocorua	121
A Whooping Indian	63	White Mountain Railway	123
An Electrical Shriek	65	Old Man of the Mountains	124
"Let go of me, Jane!"	67	Young Men's Christian Association,	
Half the Lashes fell upon me	69	Montreal	126
A Prairie on Fire	71	Post Office, Montreal	127
The Indians drew near	74	Row, Brothers, Row	128
The Child's Appeal for Mercy	75	Niagara	129
"Faster, Faster, Boy!"	77	The French Cathedral	131
Mary Bosomworth inciting the Indians		Garfield Presenting himself . Hiram	
to Violence	79	College	132
"The Light is warm on Newton's Hills"	82	Statue of Commodore Perry	133

ILLUSTRATIONS.

	PAGE		PAGE
James Abram Garfield	135	Philip Cascade	241
Assassination of Garfield	139	Yellowstone Lake	242
Merry-making	143	Mud Volcanoes	243
Gladwyn and the Indian Girl	145	Yellowstone Lake	244
Early Emigrants and their Captors	147	"Old Faithful"	245
La Salle Claims the Mississippi for France	151	Geyser Land	247
		Indian and his Bride	249
First White Men on the "Great River"	155	Hoodoos	251
Death of Marquette	157	"It's a Bear!"	254
Jesuit Fathers	159	Indian Mounds	256
The Treaty	162	Relics from Mounds	257
Union Depot	163	Pretended Finding of the Plates	258
Tower of Water-works	166	Translating the Bible	260
Palmer House	167	Brigham Young at the Great Salt Lake	261
The Little Faces seemed to Blossom with Delight	170	The End	263
		Mormon Temple	265
Chamber of Commerce	171	Grand Cañon, Looking East	268
The Lincoln Monument	175	Marble Cañon	269
Lincoln Resting	178	In the Grand Cañon	270
The State of Lakes	179	Climbing the Grand Cañon	272
Lake Como	182	Grand Cañon of the Colorado	273
Perils of Frontier Life	185	Indigenous to the Soil	275
"It isn't a Bird"	189	Mu-koori-tu-weap Cañon	276
Chit-to	192	At the Foot of the Gray Cañon	277
Emigrants on the Missouri	195	Island Monument	278
Falls of St. Anthony	198	On the Colorado River	279
Short Line Bridge	199	Palace Hotel at San Francisco	282
Falls of Minnehaha	201	In Asia	283
Hanging the Robe	203	Giant Trees of California	287
Fable Land	205	A Section	289
The Picard's Dream	206	Big Tree Tunnel	290
Land full of Ruins	207	Exhausting the Poison	291
The Spanish Cavalier	209	Prairie Dogs	293
Lake Minnetonka	210	The Yosemite Valley	295
Coureur de Bois	211	The Long Lost Brother	297
Fountain of Youth	215	Nevada Fall	299
"Three Cheers for Massachusetts!"	220	Restoration of Pueblo Bonito	303
Early Settlers in Dakota	221	Room in the Moki House	304
Plymouth	223	The Railroad crept to the Regions of the Sun	305
A Trestle on the Northern Pacific	226		
A Blizzard	229	Restoration of Pueblo Hunijo Pavie	306
Mary's Veil Cascade	236	Zuñis	307
The Grotto and Fan Geyser	237	Mining in Colorado	310
Tower Fall	239	Room in Pueblo of Taos	311
Yellowstone River	240	Garden of the Gods	317

ZIGZAG JOURNEYS IN THE OCCIDENT.

GRAND CAÑON OF THE COLORADO, 6,200 FEET DEEP.

ZIGZAG JOURNEYS IN THE OCCIDENT.

CHAPTER I.

A DISCOVERY.

THE GOLDEN EMPIRE. — A GOOD UNCLE OFFERS A FARM TO ALL. — A GEOGRAPHY LESSON. — THE STORY OF JERRY SLACK'S MONEY-POT.

HREE lads — Charlie Leland, William Clifton, and Herman Reed — were sitting in the portico of the schoolhouse for boys at Yule. It was a day full of September sunshine. In the distance, — like a jewel hung in purple, — the gilded dome of the State House at Boston shone against the sky; the gray shaft of Bunker Hill Monument rose behind it; in the opposite direction lay the Newtons, embowered with trees that displayed all the pomps of autumn fruits and foliage. At the foot of the hill where the schoolhouse stood, the river Charles wound in and out of breezeless woods and sheeny woodland pastures.

Charlie Leland was playing carelessly with a railroad map, an advertisement of one of the great lines in the West, printed in gay colors, and covered with statistics.

He laid down the map on the floor of the portico and folded it. The fold was not even, and he opened it again, casting his eye aimlessly over the bright colors of the States and Territories.

He started up suddenly.

A DAKOTA TOWN AND FARM

"Boys!"

"Well?"

"I've made a discovery."

"What?"

"I folded the map on the line of the Mississippi River."

"Well?"

"When I opened it I saw — why, it is astonishing!"

"What?"

"That the territory west of the Mississippi is as large as the country east of it, — larger."

"Why should n't it be?" asked William Clifton.

"But only a small part of it is settled. There is almost room enough to build up another United States as large as the States of the Union. Look at Dakota," continued Charlie, pointing at the map, on which statistics were printed; "four hundred miles square!"

"How large would that be compared with other States or other countries?"

"Four times as large as the great State of Ohio; as large as Great

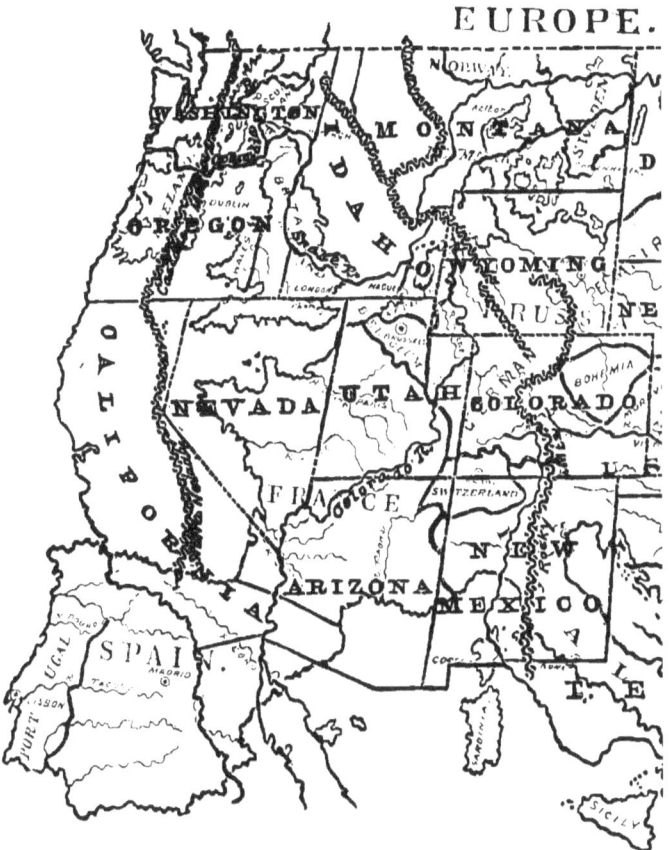

Britain and Ireland; larger than most European countries. Look at *little* Massachusetts. Why, Dakota is an empire in comparison. Then see Montana sweeping off, as broad as Germany and with no more inhabitants than are found in a German town. Why," continued Charlie, his eye still running over the statistics printed on the map, "Montana is larger than all New England and the State of New York. It contains 92,000,000 acres. It has 150,000 square miles. Great Britain has only 89,600 square miles."

"What does the government intend to do with all this land?" asked Herman.

"Give it away."

"To whom?"

"To the world. It will give *you* a farm when you are twenty-one years of age if you want it."

"That interests *me*," said Herman. "I think there is something noble in being a pioneer; in founding schools and churches; in growing up with a new place, and feeling that you are a part of it. It seems to me a more manly life than that of a book-keeper or clerk. I never enjoyed any visit to art rooms so much as I did the watching of the cloud shadows on the Franconia mountains a few years ago, and my idea of pleasure is to own a horse and carriage  and to be able to ride at will among noble scenes of nature. I have no wish to be a society man."

"That sounds very fine," said Charlie; "but I prefer a suite of rooms on Columbus Avenue (Boston) to a sod house with a big snake to make his bow to you as he comes crawling through the roof in the morning. I prefer slippers to cowhide boots big enough for canal boats, and Philharmonic concerts to the howling of wolves on a winter's night. I certainly prefer a church with stained-glass windows and full of the music of Handel, Beethoven, and Mendelssohn, to a churchless meeting in a dug-out. And as for society, I like such a reception as I attended last week. There was a young fellow there from the college who was dressed so *chawm*ingly that all the girls called him 'Sweet William,' and he bowed so genteelly that every one sighed a deep sigh, and I would much rather be a gallant knight like him than a hero of the plains. So I shall never go West to inflict any misery on the Indians. The wise general in Plutarch said that the ravens might croak and croak, but they should never have his carcass, and he marched home and left his enemies to battle among themselves. No exasperated Indian will ever adorn his belt with my head of hair. I was not born to found towns, churches, and schools. Some people are adapted to make machinery and others to keep it running: I belong to the latter class. I would like to ride over the Northern Pacific Railroad in a palace car, but have no wish to face the hardships of Western life."

SWEET WILLIAM.

"The hardships of which you speak," said Herman, "lead to good health and good morals, and make a man feel that he is living for a purpose and so respect himself. Look at the reception of last evening of which you speak, and the half a dozen swells, weak in health, in mind, and morals, who figured there. I would rather wear a patch on both knees in a manly occupation than to pose as a tailor-made man on an occasion like that."

"I did not speak of the West to advertise pioneering," said Charlie. "I prefer *little* Massachusetts, as I called the State, to all the vast Western territory. A little diamond is worth a mountain of glass."

The principal of the school, Master Lewis, had overheard the last part of the conversation and seemed interested in it. He approached the boys with a smile, and repeated some lines of Tennyson, which he meant to apply to the discussion: —

> "'Oh, who would fight and march and countermarch,
> Be shot for sixpence in a battle-field,
> And shovelled up into a bloody trench,
> Where no man knows? —
>   But let me live my life.
>
> "'Oh, who would cast a balance at a desk
> Perched like a crow upon a three-legged stool,
> Till all his juice is dried and all his joints
> Are full of chalk? —
>   But let me live my life.'"

Several other lads belonging to the school had joined Charles, William, and Herman, and had become interested in the subject; and the janitor, Joseph Mickle, had taken his seat in the autumn sunshine within hearing.

"You seem to have made a discovery," said Master Lewis to Charlie.

"Yes; I've heard that Uncle Sam is 'rich enough to give us all a farm;' but I never saw the import of it before."

"Take a map of the world," said Master Lewis; "draw from it a map of the United States, then draw upon the territory west of the

Mississippi in a colored pencil the map of Europe, except Northern and Eastern Russia."

"Would there be room?", asked Charlie.

"Make the experiment."

"Master Lewis," said Herman, "I wish you would tell us how young men may obtain government lands."

"You would oblige me also," said William Clifton. "I would like to know what are the opportunities for a young man in the unsettled lands of the West."

"What are the meanings of the *Homestead Act*, of *Pre-emption*, of *Timber Claims?*" asked Herman.

"I am glad that you are interested in the subject," said Master Lewis, "and I will try to make the whole subject as clear and simple as I can. The time may come when some of you may like to take advantage of the liberal offers which the government makes under the acts of Congress that are associated with these names. I hope better opportunities may be open to you than those offered in the public lands; but it will add to your intelligence and to your respect for your country to understand the subject, and also furnish you a good lesson in geography.

"The laws in regard to homesteading," continued Master Lewis, "are briefly as follows: —

"Any citizen of the United States or any emigrant who declares his intention to become a citizen, who is over twenty-one years of age, can secure one hundred and sixty acres of government land by filing an application and affidavit at a public land office, and by commencing settlement and making improvement upon it within six months after the application, and by continuing to live on it five years.

"Any soldier having served in the army or navy during the War of the Rebellion for over ninety days, can obtain one hundred and sixty acres of any of the public lands by filing, himself or by an attorney, a declaratory statement, and within six months thereafter filing his affi-

HEROES OF THE PLAINS.

davit and application, commencing settlement and cultivation, and continuing the same for five years, *less the time he served in the army or navy*. His widow can take advantage of the above. In case of his death in the army, his term of enlistment is deducted.

"By pre-emption, government lands are secured on very favorable terms, but under somewhat different conditions from homesteading.

IN SEARCH OF A HOMESTEAD.

"The pre-emption law requires that payment for land at the government price shall be made by the settler. The privilege is restricted to heads of families, widows, or single persons over twenty-one years of age, who do not own three hundred and twenty acres of land in any State or Territory. The lands are offered at a very low rate; the settler is allowed thirty months to pay for his farm, and he must have lived upon it six months before he can receive his deed."

"If you were to court a widow," said Charlie, "you might secure *two* farms to make your wedding happy: she one and you one. Truly there are great opportunities in the West."

"The so-called timber claim," continued Master Lewis, "is an act of the government to encourage the growth of timber on the Western prairies. It provides that any person (male or female) who is the head of a family, or who has arrived at the age of twenty-one years, and is a citizen of the United States, or who shall have filed his declaration of intention to become such, as required by the naturalization laws of the United States, who shall plant, protect, and keep in a healthy, growing condition for eight

A SETTLER'S HOME IN THE MOUNTAINS.

years, ten acres of timber on any quarter-section (one hundred and sixty acres) of any of the public lands of the United States, or five acres of any legal subdivision of eighty acres, or two and one half acres on any legal subdivision of forty acres or less, shall be entitled to a patent for the whole of said quarter-section, or of said legal subdivision of eighty or forty acres, or fractional subdivision of less than forty acres, as the case may be, at the expiration of said eight years, on making proof of such fact. I have, I think, quoted the law correctly.

"A second section of the law provides the method of making an application, and requires the payment of ten dollars on a quarter-section, and five dollars on eighty acres or less. It further specifies that 'the party making an entry of a quarter-section under the provisions of this act shall be required to break or plough five acres covered thereby the *first* year; five acres the *second* year, and to cultivate to crop or otherwise the *first* five acres broken or ploughed the first year; the *third* year he or she shall cultivate to crop or otherwise the five acres broken the *second* year, and to plant in timber, seeds, or cuttings the five first broken or ploughed, and to cultivate and put in crop or otherwise the remaining five acres; and the *fourth* year to plant in timber, seeds, or cuttings the remaining five acres.' There must be six hundred and seventy-five thrifty trees to each acre when the patent is issued."

"Can a person who receives one hundred and sixty acres under the homestead law or by the pre-emption act secure one hundred and sixty acres more by planting and cultivating the required number of trees?"

"Yes."

"Then a young man might secure *three hundred and twenty* acres of land."

"I will tell you what one might do if he were going West," said Charlie, who, after exciting curiosity, seemed disposed to deaden the interest he had kindled. "He might set out his trees and get a timber claim, then he could pre-empt, then homestead, then marry a widow who had just pre-empted and made a timber claim, and what a lord of broad acres he would be! The sun and moon would rise and set in his own cornfield, and he would figure in local histories as an original settler, and perhaps be sent to Congress. I don't think I will be sent to Congress from the East."

A TIMBER CLAIM.

"I fear not," said Master Lewis, smiling at Charlie's flow of good humor. He added, "I have the greatest respect for Western pioneers, whether they be homesteaders or preachers who ride from place to place on horseback. The future greatness and strength of our Republic are to come from such men and women. They will live in history, and ought so to live, over the mere followers of society."

"Then you would advise a young man to go West and settle?" said Charlie.

"No, not unless his taste, his ambition, his sense of duty, or his circumstances impel him to do so. I would advise the young man who can do better and be happier in the East to remain there. I would advise those who see better opportunities and fields of usefulness in the West to emigrate. Every man knows to what life he is best adapted, and I believe that every person should be true to himself

STOCK-RAISING IN THE SOUTHWEST.

and, as I have quoted, 'live his life.' The government lands are hardly intended for rich men's sons, though they are free to all." Master Lewis turned slowly away.

"I did not know that I might be so rich," said Willie.

"Nor I," said Herman.

Other boys of the school had joined the three earnest talkers.

"Well," said Charlie, "it seems as though a fortune had fallen to everybody, and I just begin to realize that this *is* a great country."

Joseph Mickle, the janitor, had listened to the dialogue in silence, but, as soon as Master Lewis entered the building, seemed eager to give his views. He was a natural story-teller, had travelled in the West, and was a great favorite with the boys. "Gentleman Jo" he was called by the scholars, on account of a poem which one of the boys recited for a declamation, which seemed like a picture of his warm, true life: —

"In the years of youth, ere the years despoil,
  When death is a word we seldom say,
  When the Hebe of health pours wine all day,
And the lamp of life burns odorous oil,
  Oh, sweet to clasp, and to clasp anew,
  One friend by the hand whose heart beats true,
  And glows with your own lost love's rare glow,
    Gentleman Jo! Gentleman Jo!

"I see your eyes of a brown so warm,
  Your deep, sweet dimples, your tossed brown hair,
  Your easeful, gracious, courteous air,
And the strong, fine curves of your manful form.
  Not a hint of the clever stuff you wrote
  In trick of collar, caprice of coat;
  Not a touch of the false, the flippant — no!
    Gentleman Jo! Gentleman Jo!

"Was there ever a man so prompt as you
  To strip all shame of its gaudy guise?
  To aim your scorn upon social lies,
  And with shafts of laughter shake them through?

When your cheek flushed up with the circling cheer,
What a happy thing was your voice to hear,
In its rhythmic richness, loud or low,
    Gentleman Jo! Gentleman Jo!

"Yet you dealt in nothing to flash or fade,
No smart grandiloquence, mock-sublime,
No dainty curse of the men, the time,
No brilliant brummagem of tirade ;
No flimsily dazzling cynic trope,
Where the egotist hides in the misanthrope,
Not the least word meant for mere bald show,
    Gentleman Jo! Gentleman Jo!

"For the love was large in your breast innate,
Your charity mild as a mother's tears ;
When you hurled at the world your trenchant sneers,
It was duty spoke, it was never hate.
And the blows were struck with a better nerve,
Since the hand that gave them was fain to serve,
Would have rather blest than have struck one blow :
    Gentleman Jo! Gentleman Jo!"

The boys also used to call him "That Reminds Me," at a respectful distance. He was so accustomed to say, "That reminds me of a story," that a part of the remark became a nickname.

The boys continued to discuss the map and the great West.

"A rainbow rises in my mind," said Charlie, with mock seriousness; "and at the end of it, as it dips down into the West, is a pot of money."

"That reminds me of a story," said Gentleman Jo. "It is one that will do you all good to hear, — applies admirably to the matter you are discussing."

The boys gathered around Gentleman Jo. The sun threw its mellow light through the woodbine which hung from the portico in masses of crimson leaves ; afar were the villages, woods, river, and mirror-like pond, and over all, the sky of a perfect September day, like an over-sea of gold. The lads took easy attitudes, and, as the shadows lengthened in the lawn, listened to the story of Gentleman Jo.

GENTLEMAN JO AND THE CLUB.

JERRY SLACK'S MONEY-POT.

Jerry — I can see him in fancy now as he used to sit on his fence swinging his heels through the broken pickets which he never found time to mend.

He was a philosopher — Jerry. He dreamed golden dreams as he used to sit among the weeds in his garden. He wondered why the Roman wormwood over-topped the corn and sent to oblivion the potatoes.

"It is the *mysteriousest* thing in nature," he used to say, — "what a different kind of luck comes to different folks in the world, *and where it comes from*. I can plan, but I cannot turn my plans into gold like other folks who do not seem to me to have near as much sense. There is always a peaked look

to things inside of my house and out of it, and yet there ain't a man in the town that likes to see things neat and trim and prosperous better than I do. This is a very mysterious world, and the poorer one grows, the more strange it all appears. Poorer, did I say? I meant older. The fact is you can't calculate, as Shakespeare says, you can't calculate; you ain't sure of anything unless you get a bone in your throat and can't get it up nor down."

A DISCOVERY. 35

The last remark was one of Jerry's favorite remarks, — one of his "wise saws," he called it. It was his way of saying that there is nothing sure but death and taxes.

Samuel Dyer was a thrifty farmer. He used to join the other young farmers after his daily work in a room adjoining the post-office and there discuss agricultural affairs. These active young men, after talking over their own affairs, occasionally gave a thought or two to the concerns of their neighbors, and poor Jerry Slack's unthrifty ways not unfrequently furnished a point for a joke.

It was planting time, the first beautiful weather of spring. The hill-sides were growing green again; the bluebirds were in the trees; there were echoes from the fields that sounded strangely clear, and a warm light in the orchards that seemed signally bright. The doors of the cribs stood open; boys were seen riding the work horses in the lanes.

After one of the mild days when everything in the earth and air seemed to prophesy of the verdure about to appear, the young farmers met in the usual place, and discussed the best preparations for sowing the early grains.

Old Farmer Martin sometimes met with the young men; he was the patriarch of the company.

"I do hate to see Jerry's land," said he suddenly, after most of the farms in the town had received due criticism. "There is his four-acre lot, it just grows up to white-weed and burdock, and it is as productive a piece of ground as can be found in the whole township."

"I know it," said James Redpath, "and that pasture of his, too. It would keep three or four cows if he would only clear it of stones, and put a good wall around it."

"And things in the house are the same as they are out of doors," said Farmer Martin. "His wife and children would hardly know new clothes by sight, and his credit at the grocer's is as worn out as the clothes of his family. I pity his children."

"I often think of Jerry," said James, "I wonder if anything short of a coat of tar and feathers would awaken in him a decent amount of energy."

"Don't let us forget," said Samuel Dyer, "that Jerry is one of the best-hearted men in the town, — generous, always willing to watch when you are sick, always says something feeling when you are in trouble. I never heard him speak ill of any one in my life; he has a charitable eye for peoples' faults, and likes to see everybody prosperous. The fact is, he's puzzled his brains all his life in trying to find out the secret of success. I could teach it in a much easier way than by tar and feathers."

"How?" chorused the other speakers.

"I have a plan; will you help me?"

"Go ahead; we'll help you," was the answer; and the result was that the next evening, when ploughing was done and the horses put up, Jerry Slack caught sight of Sam approaching his house very cautiously, hiding mysteriously behind bushes and posts, peeping out as if he wished to see Jerry, but did not want to be seen by any one else, and at last, when Jerry's head appeared through the broken-hinged door, beckoning to him to come out.

"What's happened?" said Jerry. Sam retreated, still beckoning, till he had drawn Jerry quite out of sight of the house, and into a dark corner where the eaves of the barn and woodshed met, and there at last he spoke.

"A MESSAGE FOR *ME!*"

"I say, Jerry," in a hollow whisper, "*do you believe in spirits*, and revelations, and such?"

Jerry's hair began to stiffen under his hat, for the supernatural was precisely what he did believe in, and with a very thrilling kind of faith too.

"I — why yes, I do," he stammered.

"Well, I've got a message for you from one of 'em, but I thought I'd just ask your views before I made it over," said Sam.

"A message for *me!*" said Jerry, a thrill of amazement running through his veins.

A DISCOVERY.

"Yes," returned Sam, in a deeper whisper; "a *money-pot!*"

"A *money-pot!*" gasped Jerry; "in *my field!*"

Sam drew Jerry closer to him until he had brought his ear directly in range of his mouth.

"I was — down — there!" he whispered, pointing stiffly toward a strip of woods that rose dark against the twilight sky a quarter of a mile away, "in the big hollow tree, with the scarred white branch pointing to the house where old Betty the fortune-teller died. That is the place to go if you want questions answered. Shall we go?"

Jerry glanced at the eastern sky; the edge of the moon was just visible. "Yes, come," said Jerry hoarsely.

Sam grasped his arm, and without another word they crept away toward the wood, entered it, and over crackling twigs and slippery pine needles made their way to the scarred and lonely tree.

"Hush!" said Sam, and laying two sticks crosswise on the top of a tall stump, he crossed his own and Jerry's hands above them and stood as if he were turned to stone. "Hush!" he said again.

At last the silence was broken.

There were one, two, three low, echoing raps against the inside of the hollow tree, and then a strange, muffled voice issued from the same retreat: —

"GO — HOME — AND — SLEEP — IN — PEACE — TO-NIGHT;
ARISE — AND — SEARCH — WITH — MORNING — LIGHT —
FURTHER — DIRECTIONS — CAREFUL — MIND —
AND — GOLDEN — TREASURE — YOU — SHALL — FIND."

Jerry gasped and stood silent, and Sam did not stir, but not another word came from the oracle.

"We'd better go," whispered Sam at last, and slowly and silently they retraced their steps over the crackling twigs and slippery carpets to Jerry's door.

"I'll be here in the morning," said Sam, in a hollow whisper again; and Jerry crept into the house, but with prospect of anything but "a peaceful night;" for how could he sleep in the very face of such promises of good fortune, and if he should lie awake, contrary to order, what could he expect?

However, lazy people are always tired, and Jerry slept at last, and never waked till the first streak of light from the east shone over his eyes. He sprang up with a confused idea that something had happened, and a low whistle from Sam Dyer cleared his confused recollections. He slipped the rickety bolt, and gazed eagerly into Sam's face.

"I've found 'em!" said Sam, "the 'further directions'! come and see!"
Jerry followed Sam, who led him to the great barn-door, half of which was shut, and the other half, splitting away from its hinges, swung helplessly out toward the yard. On the closed half some unknown hand had written:—

"OBEY! OBEY! OBEY!
AND FAIL NOT TILL THE LUCKY DAY!"

A line was drawn under this, and a little way below Jerry read in the same characters:—

"PLOUGH THE NORTH SIDE OF YOUR FALLOW FIELD NINETY FURROWS FROM EAST TO WEST, AND PLOUGH THE SOUTH SIDE NINETY FURROWS FROM WEST TO EAST!"

Jerry looked at Sam in mute surprise.
"But my plough's got one handle off and the prow bent," he said pitifully.
"Never mind," said Sam, "I'll help you mend it."
"But the old mare,—she's been lame these two years."
"That's bad," said Sam; "but I'll let you have my grays for a day. 'T won't do to trifle, with a money-pot at stake."
"But I can't run a two-horse plough alone," groaned Jerry.
"Well, there's your sixteen-year-old boy Tom; give him the lines, and I'll spell him an hour or two if he gives out."
"The harness's broke, too," continued Jerry; but Sam would not listen, and the next morning brought the wondrous sight of Jerry, the grays, the mended plough, and Tom, all moving from east to west across the neglected field.

The ninety furrows were ploughed at last, and yet no money-pot.
"Why, what did you expect?" said Sam. "A thing that's worth having is worth waiting for, and you're going to be led on by degrees. I knowed that from the beginning. Wait for another message on the barn door;" and Jerry went to sleep once more and waited for the mysterious disclosures of the morning light.

The oracle had spoken again. "Obey! Obey! Obey!" stood undisturbed upon the door, but this time the directions beneath read:—

"PLANT FREELY WITH THE BEST OF EARLY ROSE,
AND WAIT UNTIL THIS DOOR SHALL MORE DISCLOSE!"

"And where am I to get so many bushels of Early Rose as that there field would swallow up?" groaned Jerry.
"I've got some of my seed potatoes left over," said Sam; "and I'll let you have 'em. What's a few potatoes to expectations like yours?"

THE MESSAGE.

The potatoes were planted, but still no money-pot appeared.

"I can't stand it," he said to Sam; "I've a clear mind to borrow a spade and set Tom to turn the whole field over three feet deep. What's the use of waiting forever for what might just as well be had to-day? Spirits knows a good deal, I dare say, but 't wouldn't be strange if their notions of time were a little loose."

"Now, I'd just advise you to be a little skittish how you meddle with this piece of business," said Sam, with a warning shake of the head that pierced to Jerry's soul and marrow; "there's money in the right place now, as sure as the 'varsal hills, but once you begin going contrary to orders, and I wouldn't answer for the consequences."

So Jerry calmed down and waited again. It was slow work, but at last the barn-door glistened with fresh chalk, and Jerry found imperative commands that the earth round every hill of potatoes should be loosened and have its weeds cut out with a hoe. Once more Jerry and Tom went to work, and with many a groan from Jerry and an occasional helping stroke from Sam the work was well and quickly done. A few weeks passed, and at last, beneath the sacred "Obey! Obey! Obey!" which had never stirred, appeared directions for one more hoeing, and beneath them a few words which sent hope and courage tingling to Jerry's very finger-tips: —

"WHEN NEXT YOU FIND A SUMMONS HERE,
THE HIDDEN TREASURE SURELY SHALL APPEAR."

No more groaning this time. Jerry flew over the field with a will, his hat square on his head at last, and his hoe keeping time to such quick music that Sam's had no need to come in, and then there was nothing to do but to wait for the last wonderful revelation.

It came at last, and representatives from nearly all the families in the village were there to witness the concluding scenes.

Every one for miles around had heard some whispers, at least, of the lonely tree and the ghostly chalking on the rickety barn-door, and spades and hoes were dropped for that day, and the fence round Jerry's field bristled with almost every shade and shape of horse and vehicle tied to its posts. The last directions on the barn-door had been to begin digging at the outer lines of the field and proceed systematically, thus reducing the square by each row of potatoes in turn. The potatoes were to be made over to Sam Dyer, and by the time the middle of the field was reached, *if not before*, the treasure should be found. Sam, James Redpath, and two others had come to help. Tom was working like a veteran, but Jerry was ahead of every one of them, and making the earth fly as if the witches were there indeed.

"He's gone clean mad," muttered Farmer Martin.

One row of potatoes after another was torn open to a good depth, and the ground hurriedly examined. No treasure yet.

"Where's the money-pot? Bring on the money-pot!" voices began to shout, and faster and faster worked Jerry's spade. One by one Sam Dyer's wagons were filling up with potatoes and moving off to a corner of the field.

"Getting up to the middle row!" "Short furrows this time!" "Their hoes'll clash pretty soon at this rate!" "Look at Jerry! Sheet lightning has got into him!" were some of the remarks heard on every hand, and still no money-pot. The workers began to drop off, as the narrowing square left room for only Jerry, Tom, Sam, and Jim, one to each side.

Jerry was working like a beaver, and only three hills of potatoes to the square now. Suddenly he left his row and struck into the very centre.

Hark! Jerry's spade had clashed upon something with a sound of metal! The voices of the visitors ceased; the crowd could hear the clinking now. He stooped, pulled, tugged, and lifted something up! A wild, deafening shout rose on every side; Jerry was holding a rusty iron pot, lined with hard silver dollars, in his hands! For one moment it seemed as if the old fence would come down with the hurrahs and hat-swinging that shook it, and then there was a rush for Jerry. Two stout fellows mounted him on their shoulders, the rest fell into line, and with shouts and cheers the bewildered hero was "toted," money-pot and all, triumphantly home to the front gate of the broken fence.

JERRY FINDS THE MONEY-POT.

Great was the excitement for a few days; but after a few weeks the mystery began to clear, and a pretty plain story to rise up in its place. The ring of gossipers sat in their old place in the post-office one evening, when the door opened and in came Jerry himself.

"Look here, Sam Dyer!" he said, "hollow trees and old stumps and raps are all well enough in their way, but I'd just like to ask you if the hull of that there money-pot business was n't this: I worked like a good fellow all summer at potato-raising, and then sold my crop to you, and you gave me good market price for it, when 't was dug?"

The shout that went up was answer enough, and from that day till thĕ snow came Jerry was busy clearing the stones from his useless pasture and transforming them into a solid, handsome wall.

The next year saw pasture and potato-field both blossoming like the rose, the old house tidying up, and Jerry himself becoming such a model worker that the neighbors used to laugh as they went by, and nod to each other with a knowing wink.

"The deception practised on poor Jerry is not an example I would commend, but the lesson of the better side of the story is one which you may very profitably learn. Most 'money-pots' are found in the way of hard effort.

"'Destiny is not
Without thee, but within.
Thyself must make thyself,'

the poet says. There may be money-pots at the foot of western rainbows, and the prospect of them may give resolution and earnestness to life, but they are to be filled, if at all, with the earnings of hard labor, as was the one in poor Jerry Slack's potato-field."

CHAPTER II.

A NEW JOURNEY PLANNED.

THE WONDER LAND OF THE NORTHWEST. — GENTLEMAN JO'S STORY.

THE boys whose names we have given belonged to a school association, called the Zigzag Club. Many of the former pupils of the school had been members of this club, and some of them, who were now in college or in business, still retained their membership. Among these were Thomas Toby — "Tommy Toby" he was familiarly called — and Wyllys Wynn, a lad with fine tastes for literary pursuits. These lads had graduated from the school, but were now in college near Boston, and were thus able to meet from time to time with their academy friends.

The purpose of the Zigzag Club was to study and gain information about certain countries during the spare hours of the school year, and to visit those countries under the guidance of the principal of the school during the summer vacations. The motto of the Club was — READ AND SEE.

The first term of the year had just opened.

"What country shall we study in the Club this year?" asked Charlie Leland of the boys one evening during the first week of the term.

HORSESHOE CAÑON.

A NEW JOURNEY PLANNED. 47

"Our own," said Willie Clifton.

"The country beyond the Mississippi," said Herman.

"The Territories between the Eastern and Pacific States," said another.

"The Yellowstone Park," said a fourth, "and then go to the Yellowstone in July. I have heard that Montana is covered with flowers during this month, that the level prairies are like immense parks, and that the rolling lands are a literal ocean of blooms."

"We might make a tour through the picturesque regions of our country and include the Yosemite Valley," said Charlie.

"Let's study the maps," said Willie.

The boys look up their maps.

"I will name the places I would like to read about and visit," said Herman. "Mark them on the map with a pencil: White Mountains; Montreal; Thousand Islands; Niagara; Garfield's Tomb at Cleveland; Detroit; Chicago; Milwaukee; St. Paul; Minneapolis; Falls of Minnehaha; Lake Minnetonka and the works of the Mound Builders; the White Stone Battle-field, Dakota; the Valley of the James; The Valley of the Red River of the North; Fargo; Bismark; the Yellowstone Park; Salt Lake City; the Yosemite; the Pueblos of Arizona; Colorado; Kansas City; St. Louis; the Tomb of Lincoln at Springfield; Washington and Mount Vernon."

TREES OF THE YOSEMITE.

GIANT GEYSER.

"We will submit the names of these places to the Club, and if the Club approve our plan, we will collect some of the best books of American travel, and the newest histories of American cities and towns," said Charlie.

"I would like to confine our reading chiefly to the pioneer history of the West," said Willie.

"I have heard some news which may prove of service to us," said Herman. "You remember George Howe, one of the best and most sensible boys that ever attended the school. Several years ago his uncle went to Kansas and settled on government land. George spent six months with him after leaving school, and he is now going to live with another uncle who has pre-empted land near Frederic in Dakota. He understands homesteading, pre-emption, and making timber claims. He has seen enough of Western life to tell us something interesting about it. He is now in Boston for a few weeks. Let us ask him to read a paper on the West before the Club."

"That would be excellent," said Willie.

"But we must first get the Club to adopt our plan," said Charlie.

"And we ought to submit the plan to Master Lewis," said Willie.

The plan was submitted to the helpful teacher.

"I am pleased with it," he said. "I will send to the Department of the Interior at Washington if you like," he continued, "for the Reports of the Hayden Expedition, and for the latest information about the Yellowstone Park. This Park is probably the most wonderful region in the world. The Northern Pacific Railroad will soon reach it, and it will become the wonder-land of travellers. I may be able to take a party of students to the Yellowstone next summer."

With this indorsement the plan was submitted to the Club by Charlie, and was most heartily approved. The secretary of the Club was asked to invite George Howe to read a paper on Homesteading before the Club, and Wyllys Wynn, the poet of the Club, to give a poem on the occasion. It was voted to open these interesting exercises by singing Gerald Massey's " To the West, to the West," which the quartette of the Club were asked to learn immediately.

George Howe, in answer to the invitation, promptly responded : —

BOSTON, Sept. ——

ZIGZAG CLUB, — I thank you for the remembrance of me and for your invitation. I will read a paper at the time and place given, entitled — "How John Wyman obtained his One Hundred and Sixty Acres of Land." Cordially yours,

GEORGE HOWE.

P.S. — Should you wish it, a friend of mine would accompany me, and give you a short talk on Stock-Raising in the West. He is one of the youngest and most successful herders in Nebraska, and is a Northern man. G. H.

The offer in the postscript was most favorably received; and so Charlie's accident in folding the map led to the rather novel spectacle of a school, consisting largely of merchants' sons, interesting themselves in the study of the resources of the West, and the opportunities which the government lands offer to young men, the laborer and the emigrant. Master Lewis favored the interest in the subject, and used the opportunity with the skill of a successful teacher to secure the best results in the study of American geography and history, and especially in the unwritten history of the romantic Northwest.

The boys laid their new plan of study and travel before "Gentleman Jo." Although he was employed merely as janitor at Yule, he was a man of superior intelligence, and was very much liked by the boys. The lads often consulted him about their sports, and some of

ABORIGINES.

them were accustomed to go to him for advice on such matters as would lead a boy to seek counsel from a favorite uncle. He was such a safe and judicious adviser that Master Lewis was always pleased to have the boys consult him and give him their confidence.

Gentleman Jo was a cousin of Master Lewis. He had been a soldier in the War for the Union, and was afterwards employed as

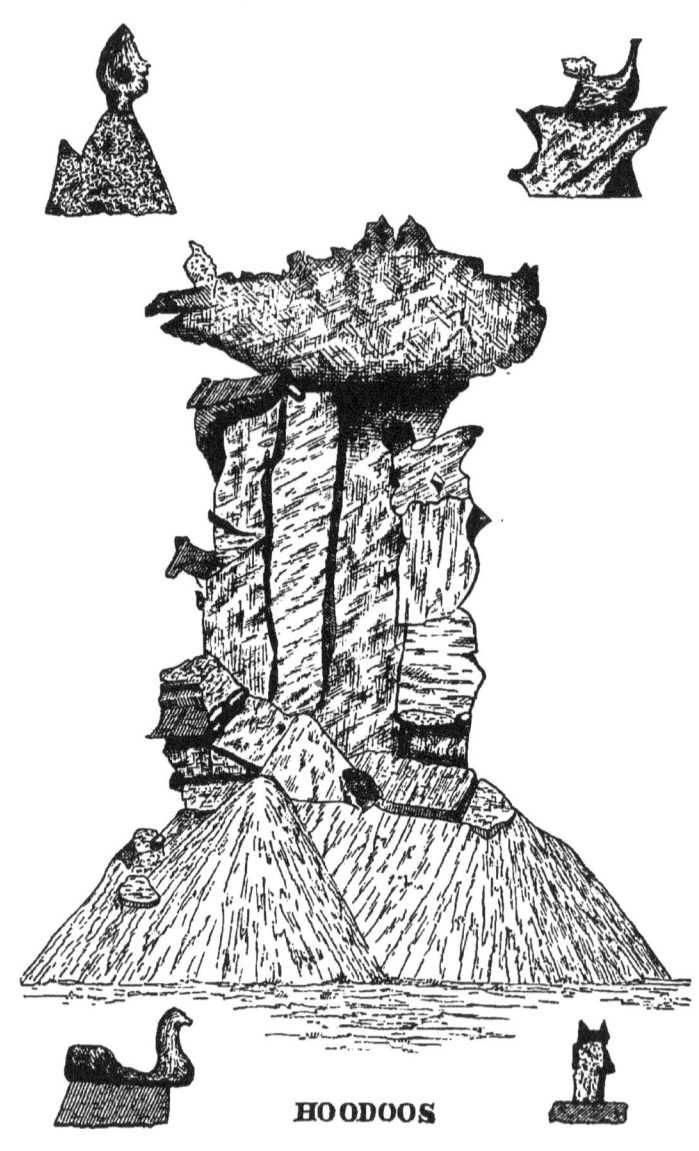

HOODOOS

one of the mounted police in Montana. He had one summer accompanied a party to the famous Yellowstone Park, and to him the region seemed like an empire of the gods. "The Yellowstone Park," he used to say, "is Nature's Wonderland."

He would usually add some amplification to this remark that would excite the imagination of the listener.

"There is no region like it in the world.

"In some unknown age it was the scene of most terrific volcanic eruptions, and the fires seem still to be burning there, near the surface of the earth. The effects of these great subterranean furnaces may be seen in the hissing fumeroles, spouting geysers, and hot mineral streams.

"It is a region of lofty mountains, yawning cañons, wonderful waterfalls, majestic petrified forests, lovely lakes, balmy groves, azure pools; of strange unions of the grand and the beautiful. When the fountains play in the sunlight, and the vapor rises over the mountains and changes into lovely colors, the traveller seems to have entered the

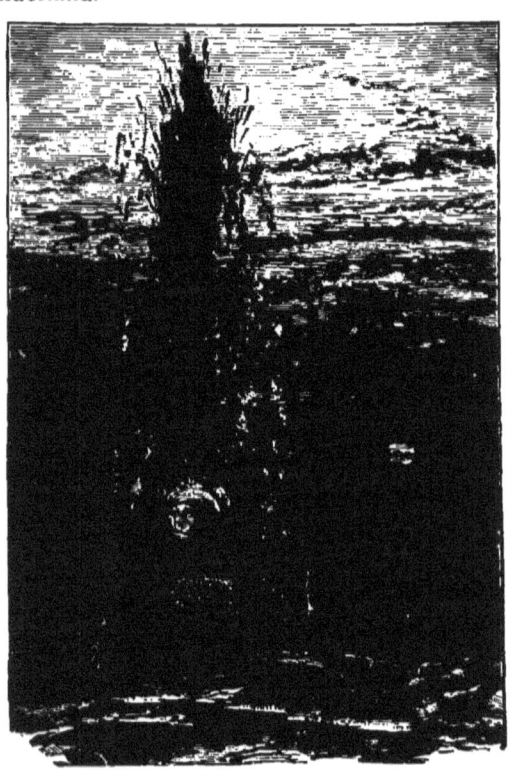

MUD VOLCANO.

land of fable, and almost expects strange beings like those described in Homer or Virgil to appear.

"There is a region there called Goblin Land, full of lofty stone monuments, the remnants of erosion, called hoodoos. These hoodoos are of almost every variety of shape. They seem to be parts of lost mountains. Lost mountains! how mysterious is the suggestion of a term like that!"

SEEDING ON THE PRAIRIE.

Gentleman Jo had suffered an injury from riding while in the service of the Northwestern police, and, being compelled to abandon the saddle, had come to Boston, and there received from his cousin, Master Lewis, the place of janitor at Yule.

Gentleman Jo had from time to time related to the boys stories of the Northwest, and these recurred to them vividly now that the Club had adopted the proposed plan of study. The boys repeated them, and daily asked him to recall new incidents of exploration and adventure.

Gentleman Jo was a very practical man. He believed in the grand destiny of the West and was full of the subject. But he conscientiously checked enthusiasts, and had no sympathy with those who regarded the opportunities of the West as mere matters of speculation. This feeling had led him to tone down the boys' glowing fancies by relating the story of "Jerry Slack's Money-Pot."

The boys used to importune him for stories of adventure, and to hint that the more thrilling such stories could be made the more acceptable they would be.

There was an innate refinement in his nature that made him shrink from narratives of this kind, much as he liked to please the boys. Yet Gentleman Jo had been a brave man at the post of danger.

"I do not wish to fill your minds," he would say, "with stories of slaying Indians for revenge, or animals for sport. Such stories tend to make one cruel and lead to a low estimate of the sacredness of life.

"I would not harm anything that lives unless compelled to," always added Gentleman Jo, after reference to the subject.

He would sometimes both please the boys and save his conscience by giving an adventure, which might have been made thrilling, a humorous turn. One of these humorous stories proved especially pleasing, and was often repeated "by request."

HOW OLD SCIPIO ESCAPED FROM THE BEAR.

I was once travelling in the Southwest, when I met a wealthy stock-raiser who invited me to his home.

He was an exceedingly generous man, fond of company, and never so happy as when he had a houseful of guests to entertain. Indeed, so well known was his reputation for hospitality that strangers had no hesitancy in availing themselves of it, always assured that they would not fail to receive a pleasant greeting and warm welcome at his hands.

Having myself often received very urgent invitations from the colonel to "come and see him," I decided to pay him a visit.

It was a lovely September morning that I mounted my horse and set out for my friend's ranch, forty miles away, which I reached about noon.

I was fortunate enough to find him at home and delighted to see me; and after partaking of a bountiful dinner, we set out on a tour of inspection over the ranch, during which I chanced to remark that I was fond of journeys into newly opened districts.

"Good!" cried mine host. "I, too, like a journey, and we'll start in the morning for a three days' jaunt. I can show you some rare scenes before you return."

"Nothing would suit me better," was my reply.

"I'm sorry that 'my boy Tom' has gone down to Galveston for a few days," said the colonel; "but we can take 'Old Scip.' He's a pretty good cook, and, although not so spry as formerly, will answer our purpose very well; besides, he can entertain us evenings, for he used to be a famous hunter in Tennessee, if we can believe his word. The old man likes to tell a story as well as any hand on the ranch. I've made him a sort of butler, a position that Old Scip's very proud of. I'll have him get everything ready for an early start in the morning."

The next day the colonel and myself, accompanied by Old Scip, in charge of a couple of mules packed with "creature comforts," started for the mountains, reaching a camping place near a fine spring shortly after noon; and after partaking of a slight lunch, the colonel and I started out on a tramp, leaving Scip to pitch the camp during our absence.

After climbing about two hundred feet up the side of the mountain, we unexpectedly came upon a large hole in the rocks, which bore every appearance of being the entrance to a cave of some size. An examination confirmed our opinion, for it revealed unmistakable signs of being the habitation of bears.

The colonel immediately sent the two dogs into the hole. After a very short time we heard a howl of pain, and one of them came out badly wounded, the other remaining in the cave.

"Poor Pont has evidently been killed, or he would have come out with Carlo," remarked the colonel. "I wish we had some way of getting at the old fellow. For my part, I don't care about going into that cave."

"Nor I," was my rejoinder. "Perhaps Scip might suggest a way."

"Well thought of," declared the colonel. "I'll call him."

In a few minutes Scip appeared in response to the colonel's call, sweating

A NEW JOURNEY PLANNED. 57

and out of breath from the exertion made in climbing up the mountain. As soon as he had partially recovered himself, the colonel said,—

"Scip, have you ever had much experience in hunting bears?"

"Sperience in huntin' b'ars, massa? Ob course I hab. I nebber did nothin' else but hunt b'ars wid de ole massa in Tennessee;" then, bursting into a hearty laugh, he exclaimed,—

"Sperience! I reckon I hab! More 'n fifty b'ar dis ole nigger hab killed, hisself."

"Did you ever find 'em in caves in Tennessee, Scip?" inquired the colonel.

"Dat's whar we allers did find 'em, sho 'nough," replied Scip, with another laugh. "De ole massa use ter say, 'Scip, you jest go in dar and fotch out dem b'ars;' an' Scip, he jest went in an' fotch 'em. Why, Massa John, one time dis nigger fotch out fo'r b'ars wid his own han's out near our cabe; fotch 'em out inter de broad daylight, too, wid dese bery hands ev, his;" and Scip began strutting about like a cock-turkey.

"Oh, they were cubs, were they?" carelessly inquired the colonel.

"Cubs? Dem b'ars cubs? No, sah," with an air of injured innocence, "dem was all *ole* b'ars, massa,—ebery one ob 'em."

"But what were four old bears doing in one cave, Scip?" inquired I.

"Da—dat's more 'n I can splain," replied Scip. "I spect dat was de b'ar's business, not dis nigger's;" and Scip roared until he fairly shook all over.

"Then you ain't afraid of bears, Scip?" inquired the colonel.

"Scart o' b'ars? No, sah! de b'ar don't live that kin scare dis nigger, nohow!" replied Scip, with another hearty laugh.

"And you'd just as soon go into a cave and drive out a bear as not?" inquired I, assuming a look of intense admiration.

"How comes yer ter ax sich a question as dat? Yer don't know ole Scip bery well, I spect;" and Scip laughed loudly.

"That's all right, Scip!" remarked the colonel. "We've found a big cave, and I want you to go into it and drive the bear out if there's one in it. Come, take this club, and be lively about it!"

Scip's face dropped in an instant, for he was evidently frightened at the very idea.

"Scip, you hear me? Take this club and go in and drive him out," handing him a stout stick.

Without offering to take it, Scip exclaimed,—

"Me, massa! me go into dat hole arter b'ars! Why, you won't hab nobody ter cook fo' you if I go in dar."

"Never mind the cooking. We want those bears out here. If you could bring four bears out of a cave for your old master, you can go in and drive out one for me."

The colonel struck the rock with a stick. The noise thus made evidently excited the curiosity of Bruin, for the next instant a large black bear unexpectedly appeared at the opening, uttering a low, angry growl of warning.

Scip saw him coming with open mouth, and started to run; but in his haste stepping upon a small rolling stone, the next moment he lay sprawling upon the ground.

Quicker than a flash he was upon his knees, uttering the most fearful cries for assistance, shouting,—

"Don't luf him come, massa! Don't luf him come! I nebber'll tell another lie's long as I lib! Oh, de lubly massa! de lubly Lord! hab mercy on poor ole Scip!"

SCIPIO'S FLIGHT FROM THE BEAR.

While he was thus shouting, the colonel, by a fortunate shot, brought Bruin to the earth dead.

Upon seeing this, Scip managed to get upon his feet, but so great was his terror that upon being spoken to by the colonel, he started towards camp. In vain did we call upon him to stop; the more we shouted the harder he ran, and when, about half an hour later, the colonel and I entered camp, we found Scip busily engaged in blowing a smouldering fire into a blaze.

"You're a nice bear hunter, you are!" angrily exclaimed the colonel. "You

A NEW JOURNEY PLANNED. 59

rascal, I'd like to thrash you for lying so about your hunting bears! You know you deserve it."

"Me lyin', massa! me lyin' 'bout b'ar huntin'! dat's de way I allers hunted b'ars."

"There are a great many camp-fire story-tellers whose narratives of daring cause open-mouthed astonishment, but whose courage in face of a wild animal would stand no better test," added Gentleman Jo.

CHAPTER III.

CHARLIE LELAND AND GENTLEMAN JO.

Wherein Charlie Leland talks with Gentleman Jo, and obtains some new Ideas about Western Adventures.

THERE are lads of such strength, decision, and moral earnestness of character that they grow in the love and respect of their fellow-pupils as long as they are remembered. Such a scholar was George Howe. He had been obliged to contend against hard circumstances in life, but he met every duty, however hard, with a spirit that ennobled him.

He had twice been abroad with the Zigzag Club, travelling in the most inexpensive way, while nearly all the other members of the Club who made the journeys were able to provide themselves with all the comforts and luxuries of the routes. But not one of the young travellers had gained more useful information than he.

He had been a year in the West. The announcement that he would visit the Club, and read a paper on Homesteading, led many of the graduates of the school to accept the invitation extended to them to be present.

Master Lewis had been consulted by the Club as to the best books of information in regard to the West.

"Begin with Parkman's Histories," said he. "Read Parkman's 'La Salle and the Discovery of the Great West,' 'The Pioneers of France in the New World,' 'The Conspiracy of Pontiac,' and 'The Oregon Trail.' They are the best works of early Western history. Parkman was a thorough scholar; he collected the choicest material from the libraries of the world, in the preparation for his histories, and his works are invaluable."

INDIAN BURIAL PLACE.

"The boys secured Parkman's Histories, and quickly followed the study of them by the reading of lighter works. Richardson's "Beyond the Mississippi" became a favorite book; also a pleasing narrative written by the wife of a pioneer editor in Kansas, entitled "The Young Homesteaders."

The programme of the exercises arranged for the first meeting of the Club had been neatly printed. It was as follows: —

1. INTRODUCTORY REMARKS . . . . By the Principal, MASTER LEWIS.
2. SONG — "To the West" . . . . Words by CHARLES MACKAY
3. HOW JOHN WYMAN OBTAINED HIS ONE HUNDRED AND SIXTY ACRES
   OF LAND; an Essay . . . . GEORGE HOWE.
4. THE GROWING OF HENRY MILLER'S HERD . . . . CHARLES WILSON.
5. POEM — "The Flag of Forty Stars" . . . . WYLLYS WYNN.

The Club was accustomed to meet in one of the lads' private rooms, but Master Lewis offered the use of the hall for this occasion, being influenced to do so by his respect for his old pupil, George Howe. He had also consented to be present at the meeting. Herman Reed was President of the Club.

As soon as Charlie Leland received the printed programme, he took it to Gentleman Jo.

"I started the interest in the West among the boys by an accident," said Charlie. "You would now suppose that the whole school were eager to

"'Cross the prairies as of old
The Pilgrims crossed the sea,'

as Whittier says. I think that the old countries are more interesting than the new, but if they are to study the West, why do they not take up live topics, not the opportunities for immigrants and young men? If the Club had invited *you* to tell us some thrilling Western stories, I should have had something to which to look forward."

"I think the selection made for the entertainment is admirable," said Gentleman Jo. "I thank you for the compliment you pay me, but let me ask what *you* would call *live* subjects?"

"Oh, rattlesnakes and bears, — the natural history of the West — Indians; I think a whooping Indian out on the war-path is a very interesting character."

A WHOOPING INDIAN.

"I think your views of the West need some correction," said Gentleman Jo quietly. "I have travelled much in the Northwest, and have never been molested by rattlesnakes or bears, and with the exception of Sitting Bull and his followers have never seen what you picture as a 'whooping Indian, out on the war-path.'"

GENTLEMAN JO'S ONLY RATTLESNAKE STORY.

"As for rattlesnakes," continued Gentleman Jo, "that reminds me of a story. I never knew but one family of settlers that had any severe nervous shock from one."

"Who was that?" asked Charlie.

"The family's name was Lamb."

"Did they find a snake in the house?"

"Well, the circumstances were rather peculiar. Mrs. Lamb, who was a very nervous woman, came home one day and found her little boy

AN ELECTRICAL SHRIEK.

on the floor asleep, with what she supposed to be a rattlesnake's tail sticking out of its mouth."

"You are joking! What did she do?"

"As she was recently from Boston, and somewhat æsthetic, she uttered a most electrical shriek and fell down in a fit."

"That was an interesting situation," said Charlie. "And then —"

"Then her husband, who had heard her shriek a half-mile away, came and comforted her."

"And killed the snake, you mean."

"No, he had already killed the snake some years previous in North Conway, New Hampshire, and had put the rattle in his curiosity box, which the child had been investigating in its mother's absence."

"Oh!"

"The woman recovered."

A ROMANCE CUT SHORT.

"Bears," continued Gentleman Jo; "there are bears in the Northwest, and some that are dangerous to attack, but the mortality of settlers from these animals is not large. I do not remember ever to have seen among the causes of death in any territorial paper, "Killed by a bear," although most of the old hunters I have met delight to tell of their narrow escapes. The fact is that Bruin is not as fond of hugging his new neighbor, the pioneer, as most boys suppose. If you give a bear a fair chance to escape he will usually do so in a very dignified and self-respecting way. I only met one young man in the West who supposed himself to have been chased by a bear that he had not molested. His name was Jerry, — not a great name for an heroic story."

"How did he escape?"

"He was a prudent youth, and so relinquished whatever impeded his flight."

"What impeded his flight?"

"A young lady, whom he had asked the pleasure of seeing to her home."

"Oh!"

"He had recently come to the West. There had been a party one evening, and bear stories had been told, and among them a hair-elevating account of a bear that had recently carried away a number of pigs from the new settlement.

"LET GO OF ME, JANE!"

"The couple were hurrying along through some timber land, when the young man heard feet and saw an object behind him."

"What did he say?"

"He said, — 'The Bear!'"

"What did *she* say?"

"*She* said, 'I will always cling to you, Jerry.'"

"Jerry ran, and the young lady clung to him, until —"

"What?"

"The dark object was close behind them."

"Then?"

"Then Jerry said, 'Let go of me, Jane; there's no need of *both of us* being devoured.'

"Jerry escaped, leaving his impediment behind him. When he called upon the young lady the next day, she seemed to be mad about something; and her father said, 'Jerry, what did you let that young donkey chase my daughter for?' They did not marry."

"You may laugh at snakes and bears, but you will hardly ridicule the Indian tragedies of the West. I have been reading the 'Legends of the Sioux.'"

"No: the Sioux war was a dark hour in pioneer history; war is merciless in almost any history, but the time of danger from such scenes is past, and the settler in Dakota or Montana is almost as safe as the inhabitants of any of the Western States.

STORY OF LONG DOG.

"I have no sympathy with the sensation stories that foster a wild ambition in beardless youths for the blood of the poor Indian. I used to know Long Dog, one of Sitting Bull's warriors, and a man whom you would suppose, from the massacre of Custer and his men, was a near approach to a brute. But he once did me a most noble favor.

"I was guarding the mail on one of the most dangerous routes in Dakota Territory at the time of the last outbreak of the Sioux, when I was captured by the Indians and taken to their encampment. I was lashed upon a mule and driven before my enemies. I received a lesson during that ride that made me an advocate of the protection of animals.

"The mule went slowly; the Indians whipped it, and half the lashes intended for the mule fell upon *me*. Since that day, or rather night, nothing has more excited my anger than to see a horse whipped. I know how it feels.

"On reaching the camp a council was held, and I was surprised to find an unknown Indian pleading for my release. It was Long Dog. I was set free.

HALF THE LASHES FELL UPON ME.

"I afterwards met this Indian and asked him the reason of his friendship.

"'Long ago him give blanket to Indian child. Him forget; Indian never forget.'"

"In other words," said Charlie, "you were in the West what you are here, — Gentleman Jo.

"What was the most thrilling adventure that you ever had in the West?" asked Charlie.

"When I was *chased*, if I may use the word, by one of the most dreadful foes that can imperil an emigrant."

"What?"

"A prairie-fire."

Charlie was eager to hear the story of adventure, and Gentleman Jo laid his hand on his arm, and said, —

"I have been accustomed to speak of this event as being *chased*, for so it seemed."

He then related the following story: —

CHASED BY A PRAIRIE-FIRE.

I was travelling with an emigrant and his family in a prairie schooner, as the large covered wagon in which pioneers move is called. The emigrant had a large family of children, whom he called Mercy Ann, Ned, Bob, Tom, Kit, and Nick. He also had a babe; to become some future Congressman, perhaps, from the West.

I pitied the mother. She was a true, good woman; nearly all pioneer mothers are.

One night I was roused from my slumbers by the children, who were awake, and the older of whom seemed greatly excited.

"O-o-o-o! I never *did!* Mercy Ann, get up and LOOK!"

A second small, dark face, the exact counterpart of the first, peered into the starlight, and another low, wondering voice exclaimed, —

"Never did *I*, neither. Ned, get up!"

Ned rolled hastily over, disturbing Bob, who leaped erect, hitting his head against a saucepan, which fell heavily into the upturned face of sleeping Tom. A terrified bounce precipitated Tom across the stomach of little Nick, who cried out distressedly, calling forth from the next wagon the query, —

"What's the rumpus, children?"

"The prairie's all afire!" exclaimed a chorus of voices. "And it's steerin' straight this way," added Bob.

"And we're so scared," said Mercy Ann and Kit, huddling close together with chattering teeth.

"Hear it roar," shouted Ned excitedly.

The father put his head through an opening at the back of the tented wagon, listened intently for a moment, and replied, —

"Fudge! it's nothin' but the wind ye hear a roarin'. The fire's miles away, and a crick or sunthin' else 'll stop its course long enough afore it scorches us. Pack yourselves away ag'in and stop yer cacklin' afore ye set the wee un a squallin', and rouse the mother up. Go ter sleep, go ter sleep," he grumbled, drawing in his head and soon relapsing into sleep.

The "cacklin'" subsided into mysterious whispers, and the little emigrants "packed" themselves, but not to sleep. Six small faces were framed within the narrow opening of the tented wagon, and the starlight quivering over them revealed a pictured medley, — blended terror and admiration, eager excitement and awe.

"It's like the *very biggest* sea on fire," said Mercy Ann.

"And the tide a comin' in on fire, too," said Kit.

"An' volcanoes busthin' up all over it," said tongue-tied Tom.

A PRAIRIE ON FIRE.

"Red 'n' yaller 'n' purple 'n' — My! I see — y-e-a-s, struc's I'm an emigrant, I do — squads 'n' squads of soldiers all afire, marchin' 'n' countermarchin'. Ye need n't giggle, Bob Fillerbuster — guess I know what 't is to march 'n' countermarch," said Ned, in a growing whisper.

"He ain't gigglin'; hesth's shakin' with skeer," interposed Tom.

"Ain't no such thing! I'm tryin' not to sneeze 'n' rouse daddy ag'in," said Bob, elbowing Tom wrathfully. "Yes, I see the soldiers now; thousan's 'n' thousan's on 'em, right down at the edge of the tide. Cricket! how their legs go! They're playin' crack the whip."

"That fire 'll rout the wolvthes 'n' snakthes 'n' prairie dogths," said Tom.

"Look! look! up yonder's all afire too. Are there prairies in the *sky?*" whispered Kit, in amazement.

Wonderful! Above the purple blackness that overhung the burning prairie burst a crimson glow. Was it a watchfire set on high to lure the footsteps of that mystic host, marching and countermarching down by the edge of the sea?

"Must be on the high land we came over to-day," said Ned. "Did ye mind how tall and dry the grass was up there? Wild hosses could n't outrun that fire. Hark! Hear that!"

"Prairie wolves," whispered the children, huddling closer together.

"Back to yer nests, all on ye!" whispered Ned excitedly, seizing the old sharpshooter. "I'll mount guard, 'n' defend the camp, 'n' watch the fire."

Kit and Nick crept into a bedquilt together, and shaped themselves into a tight, round roll, that shook like a bowl of disturbed jelly. Bob and Tom lay down upon the straw and engaged in courageous whispers, and trembled in their boots. But the distant growling died away, and only the wind made noises in the tall, dry grass. The children stopped trembling and began to wink. Pretty soon they stopped winking and began to sleep.

The stars quivered on through the night; the watchfire in the sky burned brighter and brighter; the mysterious soldiers marched nearer and nearer, while the tired little picket slumbered.

Something more than the roaring of the wind roused our sleeping senses at length. The cattle were breaking camp. The baby's face was all aglow. The fire was coming upon us. I saw that we were in danger.

"For the horses!" shouted the emigrant, in a hoarse, excited voice.

"They've broken camp with the cattle," cried Ned, pointing to the bellowing, neighing herd escaping over the prairie.

"Lord, pity us!" groaned the father, with a wild, white face. "It's comin' fast. Run fer yer lives!" he cried, snatching the baby from the mother's grasp, and driving the children before him like a herd of frightened deer.

But alas! what was frail human strength when measured by that of the Fire Spirit? Faster and faster rolled the flames, and slower and slower grew our speed. The baby became a burden in the father's arms. The mother sank breathless upon the grass, and the children dropped sobbingly around her.

"Heaven have mercy on us! We can't go no further," said the father, in a dry, choked voice. "Say yer prayers, childrun, and speak a word fer poor wicked daddy, fer he can't." A sob choked away the rest of the sentence, and the father folded his arms in mute despair, looking down upon his family with the fear of a dreadful doom written on his countenance.

But a shout of hope arising from the lips of Ned reanimated the despairing family. Right into the glow of the oncoming flames dashed four horsemen, weird and wild enough in appearance to seem the leaders of the fire soldiers, but they were human riders.

"Injuns!" muttered the father, with a gleam of hope lighting up his face.

"They 've spied the wagons, and are makin' for 'em," said Ned.

"Well, they 're welcome to all they can get; though Heaven knows all we have on arth is in the wagons," said the father sadly. "Can we make 'em hear, think ye?"

"Now boys 'll shout with ye, daddy. Now, then — Hip!" cried Ned, raising his voice lustily, joined by all the rest.

The "hello" reached the ears of the Indians. They wheeled about in the direction whence it came, listened until it was repeated, held a hurried consultation, then turned again and were soon engaged in loading down the ponies with the contents of the wagons.

"There 'll be little chance for us with all the ponies packed with plunder. I 'm afeared the red skins' greed will turn out stronger than their pity," said the father anxiously.

The fire was now hard upon the wagons, but the Indians worked fearlessly and fleetly, until a great portion of the goods were tied up in quilts and blankets, and placed upon the ponies; then leaping astride the plunder, they dashed along toward the place where we were waiting in breathless suspense. The children trembled with new terror on seeing the Indians draw near, with their scarlet blankets flying in the wind, and their dark faces making fierce pictures in the flickering firelight.

"They 'll scalp us, they *will!*" cried Kit, clinging to her mother's neck, faint with fright.

"Hush, darlin'; they 'll save your life, maybe," said the mother.

The Indians halted to reconnoitre the group, one of them counting upon his fingers the number of the family, and shaking his head doubtfully at his companions.

"For the love of mercy, save the mother and children," pleaded the father, with imploring gestures.

The Indians disputed together in unintelligible gibberish, measuring the distance of the oncoming flames, and viewing first the emigrants and then their plunder in an undecided manner. Suddenly, one of the company seemed to have hit upon a plan that was assented to by all but one, in whose breast avarice proved stronger than pity. With a disapproving grunt he spurred his pony and hurried away, leaving his companions heaping fierce execrations upon his retreating head. The remaining three dismounted, and in a twinkling threw the plunder to the ground and began hoisting the mother and children to the ponies' backs, one of the Indians holding up two fingers and saying, "No," by a significant shake of the head.

"One of ye'll have to stay behind with daddy, he means; there ain't room

THE INDIANS DREW NEAR.

fer all. Go, Ned, yer the biggest; mother'll need ye most. Which one'll stay with daddy?" said the father, in a faltering voice.

The children looked into each other's pale faces. Mercy Ann and Kit stretched up their arms beseechingly to their mother. "*I* can't! I *can't!*" cried Bob, springing frantically on to one of the ponies.

Tom, little tongue-tied Tom, who had trembled in his boots at the distant growling of wolves, stood out the hero of the night, with the spirit of a Casabianca shining in his face.

"I'll sthay with daddy," he said, slipping down from his place behind his mother into his father's arms.

THE CHILD'S APPEAL FOR MERCY.

"God bless ye, my brave sonnie! Ye'll stay with daddy, will ye?"

The Indians pointed to the baggage, made backward gestures with their hands, and the ponies dashed away.

"D' ye think they *will* come back for uth, daddy? They made ath if they would with their handths. We might run a little wayths."

"No, no, my boy; daddy's lame, ye know. We could n't get fur, and they might lose us if we left the plunder. They'll have to git here very soon if — don't ye see 'em comin', Tom? Yer eyes are sharper 'n mine."

"No; and the fire ith comin' stho fasth. If God had made a crick right over there! Maybe there iths a crick, daddy! We did n't sthee the hill. You know the alwayths mosth is."

A cry of hope interrupted Tom. "I *did n't* see it! Likely's not — perhaps the good Lord — *run*, Tommy — can't ye keep up with lame daddy? Faster, faster, boy!"

On, on, over the hill. What was there below? Only a creek making music all to itself down among the rushes at the bottom of the ravine, — but the river of life it was to the father and little boy, who soon rested safely on the other side. It was that to which the Indians had mysteriously pointed.

"FASTER, FASTER, BOY!"

The fire stopped there. From some safer place the Indians saw that it had been arrested, and soon out of the smoke they came returning the mother and babe, the children and baggage. And then, with nothing in the world left but his family, the emigrant knelt down and gave thanks to God.

"So the Indians came to rescue you and not to plunder you," said Charlie.

"Yes; and the better instincts of most Indians would lead to like conduct. The Indians have from the first settlement of America almost always been generous friends to the French immigrants and enemies to the English immigrants. Why? You have been reading Parkman, and I need not answer. The Indian has a heart for those who treat him well.

"A little captive girl was once threatened with torture by fire by an Indian whose tribe had been greatly wronged. She threw herself upon his breast and clung to him. 'I can no break heart from heart,' said the Indian: 'the Great Spirit say so.' Indian no tear heart from heart.'

"The conduct of the Indians towards the French in Canada to-day, as well as in Acadia of old, shows the force of this truth,— that even the savage respects those who trust his honor and affection.

"The Indians, and especially those of the West, have been greatly wronged. American people who have joined any of the tribes, and identified themselves with their interests, have felt the force of these wrongs almost as keenly as the Indians themselves. Like frantic Mary Bosomworth, of the old-time story, they have felt like appealing to the Indians to maintain their lands and rights against their own countrymen, so deep has been their sense of the injustice done to the natural owners of the territory. Still, an angered Indian is a deadly foe, and his passions compel civilization to treat him as such. I wish that the missionary could have had more influence, and the soldier less, in the settlement of this question of the rights of the races."

The school at Yule was an old institution, and it had long been under the charge of Master Lewis. "People exert unconscious influences," this good teacher used to say, "and I aim to bring into association with my pupils not only those persons whose habits are good and instruction superior, but those who have about them an atmosphere whose influence is elevating." He used often to quote Washington Allston's advice to his pupils: "Be pure, for nature does not

MARY BOSOMWORTH INCITING THE INDIANS TO VIOLENCE.

reveal her beauties to a painter whose mind is clouded by any grossness of character."

This aim led him to give Gentleman Jo the position of janitor at Yule, and to trust to him the general management of the house.

The boys loved Yule. The old pupils returned to it often and spoke of it as the place where they had not only received faithful instruction, but that building of true character that makes happiness and success.

THE OLD SCHOOLMATE.

The light is warm on Newton's hills,
    With halls of learning crowned;
The sunset shadow, lengthening, fills
    The memory-haunted ground.
O bowery heights! O sunlit peaks!
    My eye to you once more
Is turned, and, dim with feeling, seeks
What once it sought with glowing cheeks,
    Old class-room Number Four.

'T is autumn, and an amber haze,
    An over-sea of gold,
Is bright as in the olden days,
    And has the charm of old.
The birds are gone, the cricket sings
    Upon the grassy floor,
And quickened thought its vision brings
Of vanished youth and withered springs,
    And class-room Number Four.

I walk the upward path alone
    That once I walked with friends;
A pilgrim to the halls alone,
    My halting step ascends.
I see the pine-plumed hill-tops rise
    Around me as of yore;
Below, the weir, cloud-shadowed, lies;
Above, the blue lakes of the skies;
    The silent halls, before.

O shaded windows that I see
By pilgrim years endeared!
Where oft I dreamed, and fair to me
The future's light appeared.

"THE LIGHT IS WARM ON NEWTON'S HILLS."

Lawns, where I used to sport and play
With classmates seen no more,
Springless and summerless to-day
I wend alone life's autumn way
To class-room Number Four.

Where are they now, where are they now, —
The friends who gathered there,
And oft with faith-illumined brow
Spoke of the future fair?

Where are the ardent hands that met
  Each evening at the door?
My life is green in memory yet,
But never can my heart forget
  Old class-room Number Four.

One sleeps beside the mobile seas, —
  His life had just begun, —
And one beneath yon crimsoned trees
  Who died for Aracan.
Kind nature spreads the grass and fern
  The graves of others o'er,
The flame-tipped leaves above them burn;
Their feet, alas! will ne'er return
  To class-room Number Four.

We toil and sow, but only gain
  The harvests of our prayers;
Our hopes in God alone remain
  Of all our anxious cares.
To these, how little worth appears
  The all of learning's store,
The classic lore, the thoughts of seers,
I gathered in those early years
  I spent in Number Four.

The light is low, the sunset's glow
  Scarce hides the evening star,
And winds through dreamy shades below,
  The silver Charles afar.
Farewell! O shadow-mantled halls!
  I ne'er may see you more;
Afar the voice of duty calls,
As sombre night around me falls
  And class-room Number Four.

CHAPTER IV.

A MEETING OF THE ZIGZAG CLUB.

How John Wyman Obtained his One Hundred and Sixty Acres of Land.

THE meeting of the Zigzag Club, to listen to the paper of George Howe on Homesteading in the West, was attended by all the teachers and pupils of the school and by some twenty former pupils, among whom were Wyllys Wynn and Tommy Toby, who had twice been abroad with Master Lewis.

The exercises were opened by the singing of Charles Mackay's inspiring ballad, "To the West! to the West!" by members of the Club: —

> "To the West! to the West! to the land of the free,
> Where mighty Missouri rolls down to the sea,
> Where a man is a man, if he's willing to toil,
> And the humblest may gather the fruits of the soil;
> Where children are blessings, and he who hath most,
> Hath aid for his fortune and riches to boast;
> Where the young may exult, and the aged may rest, —
> Away, far away, to the Land of the West!
>
> "To the West! to the West! where the rivers that flow,
> Run thousands of miles, spreading out as they go;
> Where the green waving forests that echo our call,
> Are wide as old England, and free to us all;
> Where the prairies, like seas where the billows have rolled
> Are broad as the kingdoms and empires of old;
> And the lakes are like oceans in storm or in rest, —
> Away, far away, to the Land of the West!

CROSSING THE MOUNTAINS.

"To the West! to the West! there is wealth to be won,
The forest to clear is the work to be done:
We 'll try it, we 'll do it, and never despair,
While there 's light in the sunshine, and breath in the air.
The bold independence that labor shall buy
Shall strengthen our hands, and forbid us to sigh.
Away! far away! let us hope for the best,
And build up new homes in the Land of the West!"

Herman Reed, the President of the Club, then asked Master Lewis to make some introductory remarks, to which the teacher responded:—

EVERY MAN A "BARON."

MEMBERS OF THE ZIGZAG CLUB: I am pleased to know that a fortunate accident has directed your attention to the Territories of the West, and to the opportunities that are there offered to the people of the world seeking homes.

Cynical Thomas Carlyle, who did not love America, once said to a New York clergyman, "You can talk of your democracy or any other 'cracy, or any kind of political rubbish, but the cause of your prosperity is that you have a great deal of land for a very few people." Carlyle was in part right.

You have been surprised at the great size of some of the Western States and Territories, especially Dakota and Montana.

The State of Kentucky is larger than Ireland. Nevada is as large as Italy. Oregon is the size of Great Britain. Texas is much larger than France. Ohio has a larger area than Belgium, Denmark, and the Netherlands, and several of the Territories are twice as large as Ohio.

A single county in Montana Territory contains 45,000 square miles and is almost as large as the State of Pennsylvania.

But mere extent of territory would not lead to such confident expectations of great results in the future were it not for the surpassing richness of the soil, which qualifies it to become the garden and granary of the world. The prairies, which now are like oceans of flowers, will soon be waving with corn and grain, and men who would have but a poor chance of success in other parts of our country and the world will make their homes and erect their schoolhouses and churches there. The overtaxed and overcrowded populations of Europe are seeking our shores. Nearly one hundred thousand immigrants recently arrived in a single month.

When I look out upon the West and see these great, fertile, and almost empty regions, I rejoice. Not with a selfish pride that my native land has such possibilities, but for the children of these immigrants, who will find here not only free homes, but every opportunity for moral and intellectual development. These children will be the future statesmen of our land.

Look at our Congress during the last twenty years. It is a remarkable fact that a large number of American statesmen have been farmer boys and apprentices. It is also an interesting fact that these boys acquired

MEMBERS OF THE ZIGZAG CLUB.

the rudiments of their education by resolute self-denial, working at their books while others were playing, idling, or sleeping.

George S. Boutwell, James Brooks, Horace Greeley, Hannibal Hamlin, John B. Henderson, James K. Moorhead, James H. Woodworth, Henry G. Raymond, Samuel A. Smith, Silas Wright, Sam Houston, Lewis Cass, Abraham Lincoln, and many others whose names have filled less conspicuous places in American political history, were hard-working farmer boys. They earned their bread by farm labor, and used their spare hours for study.

Benjamin F. Wade, only twelve years before he was elected to Congress, was employed with a spade and wheelbarrow on the Erie Canal. But his mind was at work as well as his hands, and, with the feeling that God had given him mental qualities that should be used to influence others, he struggled until his aspirations were realized.

A MEETING OF THE ZIGZAG CLUB. 89

A number of distinguished Congressmen were left orphans at an early age, and were obliged in youth to bear the burdens that belong to mature years. Among these we may mention Augustus C. Baldwin, Simon Cameron, Alexander H. Stephens, the lamented Senator Baker, who fell at Leesburg, Stephen A. Douglas, and the late President Garfield.

Vice-President Colfax was left an orphan in childhood, and when about eleven years of age he began to contribute towards his own support and the support of his mother by working in a store.

These eminent men worked with young hands as well as with young brains. There was no sunny, dreamy period in their lives, free from care, which answers our poetic conceptions of youth. The cares and responsibilities of life came upon them at once. They were schooled in realities.

About the year 1822, in the town of Farmington, New Hampshire, lived a very poor boy not far from ten years of age. His parents apprenticed him to a farmer, to serve until he attained his majority. He was a faithful, hard-working boy, with a well-balanced mind and an eager thirst for knowledge.

YOUNG GARFIELD AT THE CARPENTER'S BENCH.

He was allowed to attend school at irregular intervals, but his school training, during an apprenticeship of eleven years, amounted only to twelve months.

No one, however, ever made better use of the opportunities for learning placed within his reach than this lad. You might have seen him reading by moonlight when no candle was allowed him.

Did he ever dream that he would one day read by the lights that throw their subdued rays over the apartments of the Capitol?

HENRY WILSON.

And how many volumes do you suppose he read in those hard years? Nearly one thousand.

Solid works they were, too,— history and biography, books of travel and of science; not sentimental novels such as dwarf the mind, deaden the energies, and lure to indolence and baser vices.

He served his apprenticeship to the farmer. He was still too poor to attend school; and having no one to assist him, his next sensible movement was to learn a trade. So, taking what few things he possessed on his back, he walked from Farmington, New Hampshire, to Natick, Massachusetts, where he hired himself to a shoemaker.

For two years he made shoes. Having earned a little money, although getting rather old for such a purpose, he was not ashamed to go back to New Hampshire to attend school.

That man became one of the most honored of the Vice-Presidents of the United States.

Members of the Zigzag Club, I rejoice at our country's resources in fertile acres, because they offer opportunities to such boys as these were, for they will plant a schoolhouse on every ten square miles of prairie. They offer to man his birthright; to labor, its noblest field; and to him who works, his dues; and better than all, they put the best education within the reach of the poor man's child. It will give me pleasure to study the resources of the West with you, and the subject will make you and me, I trust, better citizens of the noblest land on which the sunlight falls, and where every man's son, however humble his condition, is born to an inheritance which may be made equal to a baron's estate.

The President next introduced George Howe, who was received with an outburst of applause so long and hearty as to cause him to color, and to begin his essay in a faltering tone.

GEORGE HOWE'S ADDRESS.

I am to speak to-night of Homesteading in Kansas, but the conditions of homesteading are the same in all Western States and Territories.

Kansas is four hundred and eight miles long and two hundred and eight miles broad.

Its soil is rich; its climate is pleasant, the temperature in winter rarely falling below zero.

In 1850 Kansas had a population of 8,500; to-day her population is more than 1,000,000. In 1881 Kansas produced 20,000,000 bushels of wheat, and in 1880 over 106,000,000 bushels of corn.

The paper I am about to read to illustrate homesteading is a true narrative, and as an example of the most successful and thrifty farming in the West is not overdrawn.

ON THE PRAIRIE.

HOW JOHN WYMAN OBTAINED HIS ONE HUNDRED AND SIXTY ACRES.

Under the United States homestead law any person twenty-one years of age and over, male or female, native or foreign born,—married women excepted,

— may obtain one hundred and sixty acres of government land on payment of fourteen dollars fees, and after a residence of five years on the land can have a clear deed of it from the Government.

After six months' residence, if it be preferred, the person may get a deed on payment of two hundred dollars, and no further residence will be required.

Soldiers may deduct time spent in the service of the Union, not to exceed

JOHN WYMAN CROSSING THE PRAIRIE.

three years, from the five. By the pre-emption act any person over twenty-one years of age — except a married woman — may take one hundred and sixty acres of government land on payment of two dollars fees, and after residing on it six months, or for any time not exceeding three years and a half, may get a deed on payment of two hundred dollars, and giving evidence of settlement and improvement.

The timber law gives one hundred and sixty acres to any person planting one fourth of it in trees, and cultivating it for eight years. From forty to eighty acres may be taken in the same way. The fees are the same as for homesteading.

After carefully considering his ways and means, John Wyman decided to enter a claim for one hundred and sixty acres of land under the homestead law.

On looking about for the best place to settle, he visited Saline County, on the Kansas Pacific Railroad, in Western Kansas. The fertile soil, clear running streams, and unrivalled grazing facilities, with the pure, breezy atmosphere for which this land is famous, inspired him with a wish to locate within the charmed circle of the "Golden Belt," as this rich wheat country has· been poetically named.

John had no experience in Western farming. Induced by lack of means, poor health, and a desire to win a speedy independence, he had left the Sophomore class of Amherst College, to roam with whip and spurs as cowboy on the Texas prairies.

In this capacity he had served eighteen months, restoring his constitution, and gaining a small competence — some three hundred and fifty dollars — with which to start upon a life less rough, but quite as free.

Having purchased a team of stout, willing horses and a "prairie schooner," which he stocked with needful articles, John drove west from Kansas City.

He stopped by the way to call upon his sisters, Ruth and Rose, — aged twenty and twelve, — who had also emigrated from the East, and were then living with an aunt in Lawrence.

"Let Rose and me go with you, John," Ruth said, when she had joyfully greeted him. "I have fifty dollars, saved from teaching, which shall be added to your little store, and I can keep house for you, and assist you in many other ways."

"I should be delighted to take you along," John answered, "and meant to send for you as soon as I got settled; but how *can* you go now? I've got to camp out on the way, and after I reach the claim, until a shanty can be built."

"And so can we," said Ruth. "Hundreds of people camp out for pleasure, and why not we for business? Do let us go," she urged.

After due consideration,.John consented to take his sisters with him to the claim, feeling confident that Ruth's energy, sound health, and perseverance would bear her up in all emergencies, and help him to take care of little Rose, who was a child unused to hardships.

The 20th of April, 1872, they encamped beside a stream bordered with walnut timber, which furnished excellent water, and would offer pleasant shade in summer. John's claim embraced a tract of rolling prairie stretching southward and taking in a portion of the stream. Having paid his entrance fee, John began his work. There is a herd law in Western Kansas, hence he was relieved of the expense of fencing, which attends settlement in older countries.

In the first place, a cabin must be built, as the prairie schooner was scarcely comfortable in rainy weather. John bought fifty dollars' worth of lumber, which the Kansas Pacific Railroad had brought within convenient reach, and in a short time erected a good-sized shanty, which Ruth divided into two apartments with the canvas from the prairie schooner.

This completed, John began to break his land.

He prepared twenty acres the first spring, on which he planted sod-corn. After the corn was planted, John broke thirty-five acres of prairie for another man, for which he received three dollars per acre, in this way earning one hundred and five dollars of ready money.

The first summer was a prosperous one. The corn flourished, and the garden grew as if by magic, yielding delicious peas and new potatoes almost before the girls — who were accustomed to slow New England seasons — could think it possible. When haying-time arrived, John formed a partnership with a neighboring settler, and put up fifty tons of hay, which was sold, for five dollars per ton, to a large land owner who employed a force of teams to prepare his ground for wheat-culture. John's share of the profits was one hundred and twenty-five dollars.

The sod-corn yielded thirty bushels per acre. Reserving one hundred and fifty bushels for his own use, John sold the rest for fifty cents per bushel, making two hundred and twenty-five dollars on his corn crop.

A WESTERN FOREST HOME.

After the fall work was laid aside, John hired as feeder to a cattle-grower; while Ruth engaged to teach the children of the settlers, receiving her own board and Rose's as a compensation.

John's wages from the middle of November to the first of April were one hundred and twelve dollars and fifty cents. In counting up his gains at the end of the first year, John found that he had made five hundred and sixty-seven dollars and fifty cents. Of this, seventy-two dollars had been spent for sundries, leaving on hand four hundred and ninety-five dollars and fifty cents.

He now bought two good cows at thirty-five dollars per head, ten calves at eight dollars per head, and twelve young pigs at one dollar and fifty cents per head, that he might obtain a start in stock-raising, which with wheat culture affords the Western farmer his largest profit. Ruth invested in one dozen hens, paying three dollars for the lot.

Ruth did another wise thing, which I must now mention before further describing John's affairs. In 1873 she entered a timber claim for eighty acres of land adjoining John's. The law allowed her three years in which to cultivate this land, after which she was required to plant ten acres to forest trees, and the following year ten acres more, which closed her obligation to the government.

The first spring after entering her claim, she hired a boy to break ten acres of the ground, which he planted to sod-corn upon equal shares. The crop was worth one hundred and fifty dollars, and as the corn did not require tending after being planted, the boy felt well repaid to receive seventy-five dollars, while Ruth laid by the same amount.

By close calculating John would have been able to build a small frame house the second spring, but as the work upon the land required his attention, our settlers decided to make the shanty do another summer.

John now broke thirty acres of new prairie, one third of which he planted to sod-corn, to supply his stock the coming winter. The twenty acres previously broken he planted to spring wheat. This yielded fifteen bushels per acre, which sold for ninety cents per bushel. Deducting the cost of seed, — thirty bushels, — of harvesting at two dollars per acre, and of threshing at eight cents per bushel, with eighty bushels reserved for seed and family use, John made one hundred and seven dollars on his spring wheat crop.

Early in the autumn he cut and shocked his corn, and planted the forty acres of ploughed land to wheat, after which housebuilding was begun.

By doing a good portion of the work himself, John was able to erect a neat little cottage of four rooms, partly finished inside, for three hundred and fifty dollars.

The next summer — 1874 — came the dry weather, which reduced the yield of fall wheat.

John obtained twelve bushels per acre from his crop, which fortunately was harvested in season to escape the grasshoppers that followed the dry weather. With the scarcity of wheat, the price rose to one dollar and ten cents per bushel.

After saving a supply for seed and family use, John made one hundred and thirty-five dollars and fifty cents upon his wheat crop of 1874. Ruth had

A PRAIRIE SCHOONER.

let her land again on shares, having ten acres of barley planted on the last year's sod-corn land, and ten acres more of sod-corn on newly broken ground. The corn crop was a failure, but the barley netted eighty dollars.

In the fall of the same year, John planted sixty acres of wheat,—a bold venture, as millions of grasshopper eggs were deposited in the soil.

Early the next spring, however, the insects hatched and flew away to Oregon and Colorado, leaving John in full possession of a wheat-field which yielded twenty-eight plump bushels to the acre. This sold at eighty cents.

John cleared nine hundred and seventy-seven dollars and sixty cents upon his wheat crop of 1875, which established him on a secure basis. He now finished up his house, which Ruth made homelike and attractive by tasteful furnishing through very simple means. He also added to his stock of hogs and cattle, bought some farming implements, which he had previously rented, and, by hiring help, opened his entire farm for cultivation.

In 1876 John sold his cattle, for which he had paid eight dollars per head, for forty-five dollars per head, realizing four hundred and fifty dollars on the lot.

The same year Ruth harvested a wheat crop from twenty acres of her land, receiving a half share, above expenses, of one hundred and twenty-nine dollars and sixty cents. This enabled her to hire help to plant her first lot of forest trees, and also to set out an orchard of peaches, pears, and apples. Ruth bought a portion of the fruit trees, that she might have a choice variety, and culled the rest from a young nursery which she and Rose had raised from seeds, and watched and tended with the greatest care.

Ruth now has twenty acres planted to fruit trees, together with a good-sized vineyard and a variety of berries. She means to devote her energies to raising fruit.

She has already realized a handsome profit from eggs, which she has managed in the following way: When eggs were cheap, Ruth packed them in light boxes, interlaid with bran, and preserved them in a cool place till there was a demand for them in the market. She then sent them to Denver,— having obtained special rates upon the Kansas Pacific Railroad,— where they were received by a commission merchant, who returned the boxes for Ruth's future use.

During the past two years John's crops have averaged about as follows:—

> Wheat, 80 acres, 25 bushels per acre, 75 cents per bushel.
> Corn, 40 acres, 50 bushels per acre, 25 cents per bushel.
> Oats, 10 acres, 50 bushels per acre, 20 cents per bushel.
> Barley, 10 acres, 40 bushels per acre, 50 cents per bushel.

The remainder of the land — twenty acres — has been reserved for stockyards, fruit, and garden purposes.

Owing to the immense immigration to Kansas, which during the spring months was estimated at one thousand souls per day, the increase of crops somewhat lowered the price of produce.

In the spring of 1877 John obtained a title to his one hundred and sixty acres, having served out the full time required by the government. Ruth must wait three years longer, as it takes eight years to gain possession of a timber claim, but she is satisfied to work on with the prospect of being a landholder in the end.

The paper was warmly received, and added to the interest of the school in the subject.

"Did John Wyman and his sisters live on their wits during all this time?" said Charlie Leland to Gentleman Jo.

"That point might have been more clearly explained," said Gentleman Jo, "but people in a grain-producing, cattle-raising country do not lack food, and especially in districts full of game and prairie chickens. The time and conditions of John Wyman's settlement were very fortunate, and he and his sister had the *tact* that makes success."

George Howe's friend, Mr. Wilson, next read a paper on another important industry in the West.

NEBRASKA.

The Missouri Valley is in itself a matchless empire, and the State of Nebraska is one of the seeming miracles of our history. In 1855 her population was less than five thousand to-day it is more than half a million.

The State is twice as large as Ohio, and is the Ohio of the West. It is twelve thousand square miles larger than all New England, and it is a New England in point of devotion to the interests of education as it is an Ohio in enterprise.

The soil is inexhaustible, deep, and fecund, waving with flowers in the unsettled parts, and with vast vistas of cornfields as far as the eye can see in the cultivated counties. In autumn it is a golden belt of fertility, and presents one of the most beautiful landscapes to be seen in the world.

Herding is a rich industry in both Kansas and Nebraska. Let me give you a true picture of a successful herder's life and the result of his experience : —

THE GROWING OF HENRY MILLER'S HERD.

Henry Miller was the oldest of a large family of children, who lived on a farm in Pennsylvania. Accustomed to work from his childhood, without education, except such as he had received during a few winters at the district school, he grew up to manhood on his father's cold, lean, mountain lands.

On the day he was nineteen years old his father called him into the best room and talked to him, telling him of the great help he had been to him, of the hard work he had done, and ended by saying, —

"I have concluded to start you in life on your own account. You can stay here among the mountains on a farm if you wish, or you can go to the West, say to Nebraska or Kansas, and there farm to grain, or raise cattle, just as you see fit. When you have decided where you will go, let me know and I will do my best for you. I can let you have five hundred dollars, not more, but I have some valuable advice for you if you go West."

Henry thought over the offer, and finally concluded he would go West, but whether to farm or raise cattle, he did not decide. He notified his father of his decision, and they had a long conversation.

The father was a man of great good sense, and Henry received the best advice. In substance he said, —

"You will find in Kansas and Nebraska great tracts of land, owned by Eastern men who bought the land on speculation. This land is known as the Speculators' Land. There are no homesteaders there, and the land is free to all to graze their cattle.

"Raise cattle. Do not own real estate. You can drive your cattle to market, and not pay a cent for freight to any railroad. There are no expensive machines used in cattle-raising. You do not have to pay harvest hands three dollars per day. You can start your cattle for another State at an hour's notice. You can hold over a year's stock if the price does not suit, and the quality of the stock will be improved by the holding.

"Do not let your head be turned by the beautiful land you will see. Do not get greedy for real estate, but when you get there hire to some stock-dealer as a herder; pay attention to what you see; learn the business of raising cattle, of feeding them; then invest your money. Don't marry until you get your start in life."

This was in May of 1868. By the last of May Henry was in Nebraska. Here he succeeded in getting work from a cattle-dealer, who had just arrived with a big herd of beeves and stock-cattle from Texas. As a herder, Henry was to be paid twenty-five dollars per month, with board, and a pony and saddle furnished him.

Here Henry was instructed in the art of herding, was cautioned against running the cattle, was told that his duty was simply to keep the cattle in sight, to let them have their own way as much as possible, not to let them get lost, and when the sun was low to help to drive them slowly to the bed ground, there to watch them.

Henry had to take his turn "herding o' nights," and during storms the entire force of herders would be out. If a fierce wind storm accompanied by rain or hail sprang up in the night, Henry had to ride around the bed ground with the other herders, singing, so as to let the cattle hear the human voices, thus endeavoring to prevent the dreaded stampede the cattle of Texas are subject to.

ROUNDING UP A HERD.

On November first he was hired by the owner to help herd and feed a "bunch" of steers he intended to hold over the winter. And here he learned how to winter-herd cattle, a distinct thing from summer herding. Though exposed to the cold north storms that sweep over the Western plains in the winter, known as "Blizzards," he kept his health, and in a year he had earned three hundred dollars. His expenses for railroad fare and clothing had been one hundred dollars. So he now had seven hundred dollars.

On the first of June he again hired to a man from Texas for twenty-five dollars per month, until the first of November.

During July he hired two settlers to cut and stack forty tons of hay for him; he showed them where to stack it in a bend of a river, where the timber afforded some shelter, and where the water flowed rapidly, so that it would not freeze during the winter. The settlers stacked this hay for two dollars per ton of three hundred and forty-three cubic feet, to be measured when the stack was settled, and ploughed a fire guard around it.

During the summer, while herding, Henry became acquainted with the character of the cattle under his care. He studied the two-year-old heifers under him, and by the first of November he had selected forty two-year-old heifers that did not stray away from the herd while feeding, that were short of leg and large in

THE HERDER'S HOME.

body, and that were comparatively gentle; for these he paid ten dollars per head. Henry paid eighty dollars for hay, four hundred dollars for his heifers, and twenty dollars for clothing, a total outlay of five hundred dollars. He had earned during the summer one hundred and twenty-five dollars. So he, in the fall of 1869, had forty heifers and three hundred and twenty-five dollars in cash.

That winter he tended his cattle and helped the settlers husk corn, chop wood, and do their chores for his board. By the first of April he had thirty-six calves. By the first of May he had hired to a man who owned a herd of cattle, as a herder for twenty dollars per month, he to be allowed to put his cattle in the herd free of charge.

During the summer he had sixty tons of hay stacked in the same bend of the river. For this he paid two dollars per ton. He paid one hundred dollars for some choice stock, one hundred and twenty dollars for hay, twenty dollars for clothing, and twenty-five dollars for a pony and saddle, — a total outlay of two hundred and sixty-five dollars for the year. He earned one hundred and twenty dollars; so he had seventy-seven head of cattle and one hundred and eighty dollars in cash.

The history of the summer of 1871 was similar to that of 1870, and that fall found him with one hundred and seventy-four head of cattle.

In 1879 Henry Miller owned nine hundred and thirty head of cattle, four ponies, a team of horses, and a wagon, but not a foot of land. He must have been worth more than ten thousand dollars.

"I would not recommend a young man to start in life as a herder," said Gentleman Jo to Charlie; "there are privileges in society from which one cannot afford to be wholly separated. Still, the business is honorable and useful."

"Are there any questions that members of the Club would like to ask?" inquired the President.

"Will Mr. Howe tell us how grain is harvested on the great farms of the West?" asked Master Lewis.

"In the valley of the Red River of the North," said George, "and about twenty miles from Fargo, Dakota, is the farm of Mr. Oliver Dalrymple. It was, as I saw it a few weeks ago, an almost solid wheatfield of some twenty-six thousand acres. Over it were waving more than five hundred thousand bushels of grain. The superintendent employs in the harvest season more than one hundred self-binding reapers and twenty steam threshers.

"I went out one morning from Fargo on the Northern Pacific Railroad, and looked out on this ocean of grain shining in the clear, dry air and bright sun. All was life and energy about the place. Superintendents were putting divisions of men, animals, and machinery in readiness for reaping. It seemed like the mustering of an army. Into the field these divisions rode, a nobler field than many that are famous in history, and the grain fell before these chariots of peace, and I thought of the history of the past, and I said, Thank God this is America!

DALRYMPLE FARM.

A MEETING OF THE ZIGZAG CLUB.

"I returned to Fargo at night. Ten years ago there was no Fargo. In 1879 it was a city in outline. I found it a city crowned with spires and towers of churches and schools, and in the sunset the sound of the hammer was still busy, a better note than any drum tap of war, and I said again, Thank God this is America!"

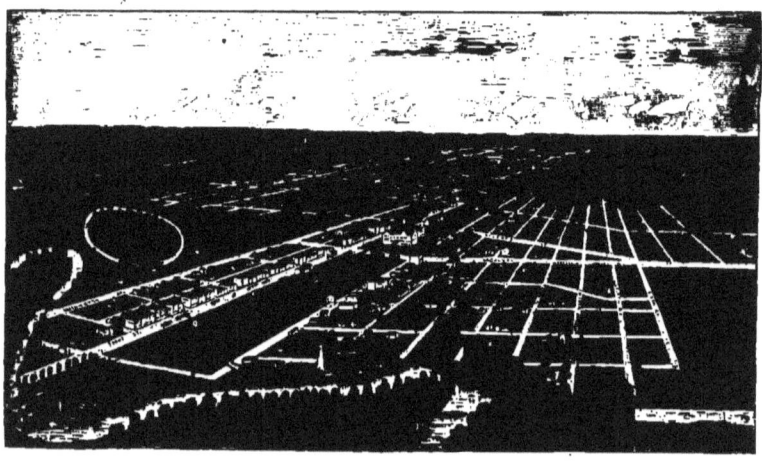

FARGO, DAKOTA TERRITORY.

"He's getting patriotic," said Charlie to Gentleman Jo. "Does it make one feel like that to travel through the West?"

"It affected me that way," said Gentleman Jo.

"I am glad we have a patriotic poem to close our exercises," said the President, bowing to Wyllys Wynn, who rose and read: —

THE FLAG OF FORTY STARS.

I walked in Arlington's lone fields near even :
  The wings of Night drew nigh ;
While half the sun, like a far gate of heaven,
  Burned in the autumn sky.

No more the lawns with fountain spray were christened;
  But, 'neath the glimmering domes,
Far in the purpling light the city glistened,
  A wilderness of homes.

On crisping leaves was Nature's pen inditing
  The lesson of the fall,
Seeming almost like that mysterious writing
  In Babel's banquet-hall.

Around me rose white monuments in clusters,
  An open space before,
Where graves reflect few monumental lustres, —
  A sad field of Manoah.

It is the field of single graves, where slumber
  Young heroes 'neath the mounds;
And yet "Unknown" on tablets without number
  I read in those broad grounds.

There heroes sleep. Balm-breathing Junes returning
  Touch with wild flowers their bed;
And fair years pass with golden harvest burning,
  Above the unknown dead.

They hear no more the hollow bugles blowing
  On Freedom's natal days,
Nor catch the strain in sweet, suave numbers flowing,
  That speaks the patriot's praise.

To think of them the gay world seldom pauses;
  They had in it no part;
In life they gained no feverish applauses,
  In death, no shaft of art.

I said to one I met, a soldier lonely,
  With sorrow in my eyes,
"Brave men lie here;" and then I added, "Only
  How great the sacrifice!"

Toward the Potomac and the Capitol turning,
  Then said the man of scars,
"I see, amid the twilight hazes burning,
  The Flag of Forty Stars.

"The blue Potomac hears no battle-marches;
The fruiting fields increase;
And Plenty piles her stores to heaven's arches,
And all the land is Peace."

Night's curtain fell, the distant city shading:
I left the field of Mars;
But long I saw above the Capitol fading
The Flag of Forty Stars.

After the reading of the papers and the poem Master Lewis was asked by the President, in behalf of several pupils, if he would take a party of his pupils through the Western Territories during the next summer vacation.

"I expected the question," he answered, "and am prepared to answer it. If my health continues good, I will take a party of my pupils to the Yellowstone Park next summer, and perhaps to California, returning by the Southwestern route through Colorado. I look upon the plan so favorably that I would advise the members of the Club to continue to read the best books that give information about the West, which it requires no prophet to see is the world's new empire. The works of Schoolcraft, the Reports of the Lewis and Clark Expedition, Greeley's 'Overland,' the Earl of Dunraven's 'Great Divide,' the Report of the Hayden Expedition, and even Mark Twain's 'Roughing It,' are a few of the books I would recommend. I am sorry that only a few pupils will be able to go on the excursion, but it will do all alike good to study the subject."

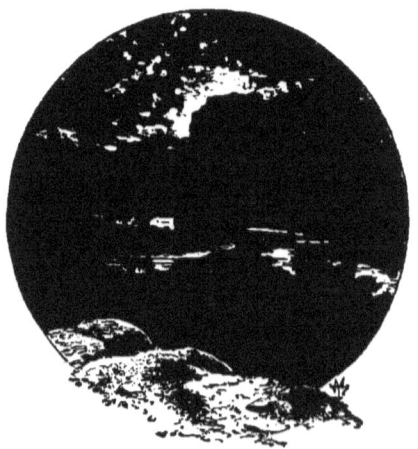

108   ZIGZAG JOURNEYS IN THE OCCIDENT.

This cordial expression of sympathy with the aims of the Club was received with applause.

"As the party will visit Minneapolis," said George Howe, "I hope you will make a detour and visit Brown County, Dakota, where you may have a view of a new settlement, in which I shall do my best to become a good citizen and prove myself worthy of my teachers, classmates, and the excellent academy at Yule."

CHAPTER V.

A STORY-TELLING JOURNEY.

BOSTON. — PARSON POOL'S MIRACLE. — MONTREAL. — TOM MOORE IN AMERICA. — NIAGARA. — GARFIELD'S TOMB.

T was June, a time when the suburbs of Boston are among the most lovely of any city in the world.

"I have arranged the journey from Boston to Chicago," said Master Lewis to the Zigzag Club on the occasion of their last meeting before the summer vacation. "The route is through the most picturesque scenery in the East. Our party will go by the way of Alton Bay, Lake Winnipiseogee, and the Ossipee stages to North Conway, New Hampshire; through the White Mountains, and by the St. Albans and Lake Champlain route to Montreal. We will then go up the St. Lawrence to Toronto on the Lake; thence to Niagara, and thence by rail along the shore of Lake Erie to Cleveland and Detroit; thence to Chicago, at which point our Western tour may be supposed to begin. This route will afford the finest views of the mountain and lake scenery of the East, and will prepare us for the contrasts of the West."

The party consisted of seven persons: Master Lewis and Gentleman Jo, Tommy Toby and Wyllys Wynn, Herman Reed, William Clifton, and Charlie Leland. Gentleman Jo took the general management of the excursion.

Tommy Toby and Wyllys Wynn, as we have said, were former pupils of the school, but still continued their membership of the Club.

STATE HOUSE, BOSTON.

The excursionists called themselves THE CLASS, and so we call them in this volume.

Gentleman Jo was engaged to explain the associations of places to the Class, and, as he usually imparted instruction by story-telling, his selection for the purpose was very pleasing. Wyllys Wynn had the faculty of turning incidents of travel into rhyme, and it afforded him as much pleasure to do so, as it gives a travelling artist to sketch and paint.

Early one June morning, when the Public Garden was full of birds and roses, and the Common was a broad canopy of dewy leaves, the party crossed the city of Boston from the Columbus Avenue station, and were soon swept away from the Eastern Depot for Alton Bay. The afternoon found them on Lake Winnipiseogee, and the evening of the long day, in North Conway. The sail on the lake had brought to view long ranges of pine-covered hills in the serene sunlight of a late June day. The ride in the Ossipee stage enabled them to approach the White Mountains gradually, and as the peaks grew higher, and the shadows of the fragrant pine forests lengthened in the approaching twilight, the beauty above, below, and on every hand was fraught with the charm that so often awakens feelings never experienced before. Beautiful villages nestled among the hills, and little red houses scattered here and there adorned the intervales.

STATUE OF EDWARD EVERETT.

The old stage-driver of Ossipee was a story-teller. The boys all desired to ride outside of the coach, and they might well do so, for no

THE OSSIPEE STAGE.

ride can be more exhilarating than one on an old-time stage-coach through the Ossipee hills.

The stage-driver related to the boys several stories of the towns on the route. One of them presented such a picture of rural life in the White Hills that we give it, though in part in different language, here. He sat in an easy attitude, with the whip in one hand and the reins hanging loose from both hands. He hardly smiled, but spoke as though there was something sad in recalling old days, even in relating a funny story.

PARSON POOL'S MIRACLE.

For fifty years Parson Pool had faithfully served the little parish among the New Hampshire hills. There was not a house in the village in which he had not prayed; there was hardly a little red cottage on the road that wound through the intervale in which he had not at least "married one and preached the funeral sermon of two," as he expressed himself in a discourse at the close of the half-century of his ministry.

There had been but few episodes in the parson's life. He had seldom travelled so far as to lose sight of Mount Washington, or not to hear on Sunday the ringing of his own church bell. Week by week on Friday evening and Sunday morning, his strong form was seen passing through the wicket gate that led to the church, whether the breath of June was in the air, or Chocorua's triple peaks were obscured by a scowling sky, or rose in silence, covered with snow. But in his old age there happened to him a *miracle.* I myself saw it, though I was then a child.

Parson Pool was my grandfather. I was his pet. He used to take me with him to his parishioners whenever he went. I well remember his gig and poor old Dolly, the mare, with her harness all tied up with tow strings and toggles, — a faithful animal who bore her lashings with resignation, and has long been free from her woes.

Parson Pool was a very tender-hearted man, and next to his love of children was that of animals, notwithstanding the whacks that old Dolly received.

There used to be a season in the village which was called " killing time, " — a few weeks in December when the fatted cattle, hogs, and poultry were killed. The neighbors used to gather from house to house on the occasion of such annual slaughters, but the parson was never seen among them. He usually shut himself up in the garret on the morning that his own pig was killed, and did not appear below stairs until the defunct animal's "liver and lights" were frying for the butcher's dinner. If he were riding at this season and heard one of his neighbor's pigs squeal on being run down by the butcher, he would give old Dolly an extra whack, put the reins between his knees, and clap both hands over his ears, and hold them there tightly.

"Mary," I once heard him say, after such an experience, "it does seem to me that there is something wrong in the make-up of this world; but then," he added, "I ought not to say anything, — I like a piece of fresh pork myself sometimes."

The people generally remembered the parson at "killing time," and generously sent him spareribs, turkeys, and geese. He was so well provided for with poultry at this season by others, that he was never known to kill any of his own.

"I would n't kill a chicken," he used to say, "if I had to live on corn bread all the year. I sell all my poultry to the hen-cart."

Just what the hen-cart man did with the parson's poultry, the good man never cared to investigate. The hen-cart always went outside of the mountain hemlocks that bordered the quiet town.

THE PEOPLE GENERALLY REMEMBERED THE PARSON.

Grandmother Pool was a person of different fibre. At "killing time" at the parsonage, she went round with her sleeves rolled up, ready for the fray. When she mounted the gig, and said "Go lang," old Dolly put back her ears, and her stiffened legs flew like drumsticks. Grandfather used to have to speak to me about the same thing often, but I very distinctly remember that grandmother, after giving me one or two very impressive lessons, never had to speak to me in that way but once. Grandmother was *not* a popular woman in the parish.

Parson Pool liked to raise poultry. He would often bring up a large brood of chickens by hand, and his flock of hens would follow him about the farm whenever he went out to walk. In the summer afternoons we used to go up on a hill together, which commanded almost as fine a view of the green mountain walls and the bald summits of Washington and Lafayette as does the Bald

Mountain itself. Then we would sit down and watch the shadows of the clouds on the pine-covered mountain sides, as they sailed along like ghosts of the air. When Grandmother Pool asked us where we were going, as we set out for these excursions, he would often answer, " Hens' nesting."

A mania had spread over the country. It was called the " hen fever." It reached at last our village. Several people became the possessors of Cochin China and Shanghai hens, and among them was a brisk young farmer by the name of Campbell.

Just after Thanksgiving this young man summoned Parson Pool to marry him. He paid the old man two dollars in money, and promised to make him a present of a Christmas dinner, which he assured him should be "a surprise."

It had been an open fall. October had been full of crimson and golden foliage, and the mountain walls of Crawford Notch a blaze of glory from the ravine to the sky. I had ridden through the Notch one day with grandfather, and, as we jogged along the dreamy ways in which the crisp leaves were falling, he had told me the story of Nancy's Brook, and he had pointed out to me the place where the poor girl perished, which is near where Bemis's Station is to-day. November found Washington white with snow, but with a summer loveliness in the intervales; and with the exception of a few sharp, gusty days, the beautiful weather lasted until the day after Christmas.

On the day before Christmas young Campbell had called at the parsonage, and had fulfilled his promise. It was a surprise indeed, — a Shanghai chicken of astonishing weight, and seemingly fabulous length of neck and legs.

" Here, parson," said he, setting the pullet down on the kitchen floor, " I 've brought you something for your Christmas dinner. Big as a turkey, ain't it? Legs almost as long as yours, parson, and a neck like as it was going to peek over the meetin' hus' into the grave-yard. Did you ever see the like of that?"

The chicken ruffled its feathers, and walked about the kitchen very calmly, lifting high its feet in a very dignified way.

"'When this you see, remember me,' parson," said the lively young man, quoting provincial poetry, "You will have *him* on the table to-morrow, won't you, parson?"

"Yes, but, but —"

The old man held out a piece of bread. The pullet walked up to it like a child, and swallowed it so fast that it choked desperately.

"But what, parson?"

The pullet wiped her bill on grandfather's dressing-gown, which seemed to please him greatly.

"But I would kind o' hate to cut her head off."

"Is that so, parson? Well, I'll save you the trouble. You just let me take your hatchet, and I'll—"

"No, no," said grandfather, with a distressed look, "I'll attend to the matter. I'll attend to the matter. I always was kind o' chicken-hearted, myself."

"HERE, PARSON."

After the young man left, grandmother came upon the scene, with a resolute look in her face and her cap borders flying.

"Samuel!"

"Well?"

"I want you to cut that chicken's head right off, right off now, so that I can have it to bake for breakfast to-morrow. Who do you think is coming to spend Christmas with us? Sophia,— Sophia Van Buren, from Boston. She spent the summer at the Crawford House, and came to the mountains again in October. But now that the hotels are closed, she is coming here."

"What is *she* coming for?" asked grandfather, with a distressed look at the chicken.

"To see Mount Washington covered with snow. She is an artist; she exhibits pictures in the art rooms in Boston. She is my second cousin."

"When is she coming?"

"This very afternoon in the Ossipee stage. So just take that great fat chicken, and off with its head just as quick as you can, and I will get the feathers out of the way in half an hour."

"But I never killed a chicken in my life, and I would rather hate to hack the head off of such a fine-looking bird as that."

"Won't she *brown* up well?" said grandmother.

"Rebecca, that fowl loves to live just as well as you do. Just think of it, when the day-star rises to-morrow and the cocks crow, she —"

"Will be dead and baked in the larder," said Grandmother Pool.

"And when the sun rises and the other fowls are enjoying the sunlight —"

"You will be eating one of the best roast chickens you ever tasted. Here she is," added grandmother, catching up the plump pullet and handing her to Grandfather Pool, who looked as though he had been called upon to execute a child.

Grandfather Pool went out with the pullet, which did not seem to manifest any concern. I followed. He went to the woodhouse where the chopping-block was, and sat down in an old arm-chair, in the sun. The woodhouse was open in front, and the chopping-block stood in the opening.

"Are you really going to do it?" said I.

"I wish one of those Old Testament miracles would turn that pullet into a chopping-block, for *she* has said it must be done, and nothing but a miracle will ever save the poor thing from the *gallows*."

Grandfather Pool rose up and laid the chicken on the block. He measured the distance with the hatchet.

"Oh, let me run," said I.

"I am not going to do it yet," said he. "When I do, I shall measure the distance *so*, with my eyes open ; then I shall shut my eyes tight, chop her head off quick, and throw her away, and shall not open my eyes until she is as dead as a stone. Now you run away, and write the epitaph," he added, with a grim smile.

I ran to my room. It looked out on the woodhouse. I drew the curtain so as not to see the awful sight. I began to think of the epitaph.

There was a nice fat pullet that sat upon a roost;
Death came along and gave her a *boost*.

That did not seem quite correct.

There was a nice plump pullet that lay beneath the brier;
Death came along and caused her to expire.

This seemed to me perfectly lovely, and I felt willing that the pullet should die, that she might be honored by such an epitaph. Parson Pool was famous as a writer of epitaphs, and I now felt sure I had inherited his genius.

I thought I would just open the curtain to see if the deed was done, when a most remarkable sight met my eyes. Grandfather Pool stood by the block on which the pullet was laid, measuring the distance to strike. He then shut his eyes, brought down the hatchet strongly, and threw the pullet away. What was my astonishment to see the fowl jump up and run across the meadow into the hemlocks.

Grandfather stood like a statue, with closed eyes, waiting for the pullet to expire. I think he stood in this position some five minutes, when he ventured to look slowly round.

There was nothing to be seen but the chopping-block.

He walked around it, and then surveyed the yard. I never saw such a look of astonishment as came into his face.

Presently I heard a shrill voice cry, —

HE SHUT HIS EYES AND THREW THE PULLET AWAY.

"Samuel, ain't that chicken ready yet?"

Then I heard him say, —

"Rebecca, come here."

"Where is the pullet, Samuel?"

"I chopped her head off, when she vanished right into the chopping-block. It is a punishment for my sins. I never thought it quite right to kill innocent animals for food."

"Samuel, have you lost your senses? I am not a fool. You never cut that pullet's head off in this world. It stands to reason you did n't; there is n't a drop of blood on the block."

"Rebecca, I have never told a lie since I entered the ministry. I tell you the truth: I cut that pullet's head off; the hatchet went clean through her neck, when she vanished head and all, — went right into the chopping-block!"

"Split open the block and you will find her, then."

Grandfather took up the broad-axe, severed the chopping-block in the middle, and examined it carefully as it fell apart.

"There is no pullet there," said he. "I feel like Balaam. I've read of such things in books, — they happened to Samuel Wesley, and he was a good man; and to Elder John Leland, and he was a good man."

"What things?"

"Supernatural things, — miracles, like."

"Well, I don't believe in them."

"What's come of that pullet, then?"

"Did n't you fall asleep over the chopping-block, and some one steal her?"

"Rebecca, you know that there is n't a person in this whole town who would steal a hen from me in the night, to say nothing of broad daylight. What's the use of arguing against the supernatural? Just as soon as I had cut her head off, I let go of her, and expected she would flutter and leap up into the air, just as pullets do when other folks kill them. Instead of that she never made a sound, but turned right into that there chopping-block, and never left so much as a drop of blood or a feather behind."

"It is very mysterious."

"Very."

"Where's Jamie?"

"He's hid so as not to see the *murder*."

Just then the sound of wheels was heard, and the Ossipee stage stopped before the little red cottage, and Miss Van Buren, all fluffs and furbelows, appeared. As soon as I was alone with grandfather he said, —

"Jamie, you know what has happened; don't tell your grandmother that rash wish of mine."

"What wish?"

"What I said to you before the pullet vanished,— that she might turn into a chopping-block."

I had intended to tell him what I had seen, but a mystery had a charm for me even in childhood. I disliked to spoil such a famous story as this was sure to become, and when my conscience began to trouble me, I stifled it by reflecting that to explain the matter too soon would cause the capture and death of the pullet.

HE EXAMINED IT CAREFULLY.

The next day, a wonderfully mild Christmas in that region, grandfather, Miss Van Buren, and myself went up the high hill to get a view of the mountains. I shall never forget the scene. It seemed like an ocean of mountains, and the snow on the highest peaks looked like foam on the majestic billows. The Saco River was seen winding away through leafless trees and past groves of dark pine, looking afar like a ribbon of silver. Winnipiseogee Lake lay in the distance, a sea of splendor. The sharp peaks of Chocorua seemed to cut the air, and grandfather told Miss Van Buren as we slowly went along the awful story of Chocorua's curse. Had I not known the true explanation to the pullet story this story of

CHOCORUA.

the old Conway farms would have chilled me, for the Conway farmers believe that Chocorua's curse causes the cattle to die. The air was very still, only a low murmur at times in the tops of the pines.

There were hunters in the woods below us, and from time to time the crack of a rifle would cause us to stop to listen to the echoes. As we returned I hurried ahead of grandfather and Miss Van Buren, and gained the highway some minutes before them.

A wagon was passing, full of hunters and game. Out of one

of the game bags hung the head of a noble bird; my eyes recognized it with astonishment, — it was Parson Pool's Christmas pullet.

The next day the Class passed through the White Mountain Notch. It was early morning. The pine-covered mountain walls were overhung by a cloud of mist that floated, bright and billowy, like a sea in the unseen sun. Gentleman Jo related to the Class the wild legend of Chocorua, and the stories of Nancy's Brook and of the Willy House. The party lunched at Fabyan's, then passed up into cloud-land by the Mount Washington Railroad, and looked down upon picturesque New England from Mount Washington.

WHITE MOUNTAIN RAILWAY.

The late hours of the day found the Class on the Central Vermont Railroad in view of the glimmering waters of Lake Champlain, and crossing the monotonous Canadian flats. At this latter part of the route Gentleman Jo took occasion to relate the wonderful story of the building of the Victoria Bridge over the St. Lawrence near Montreal, and of the four thousand emigrants who died there of ship fever at the time and were buried in one small lot in the beautiful city.

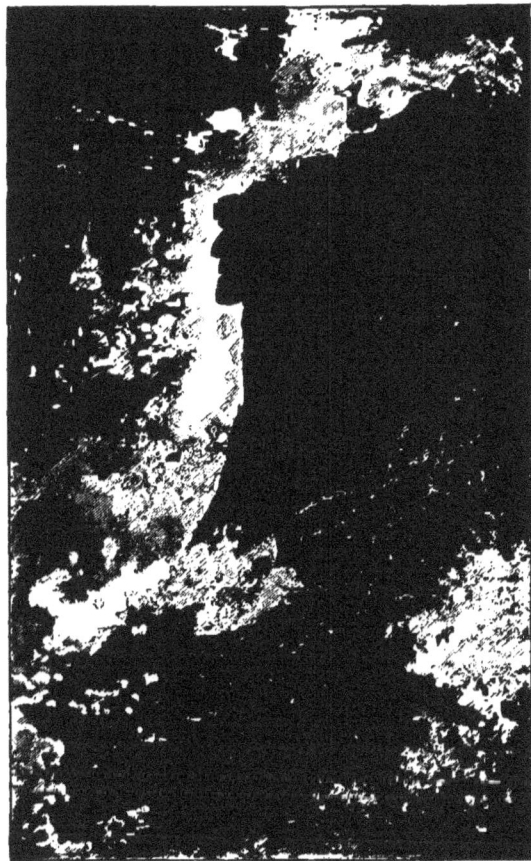

OLD MAN OF THE MOUNTAINS.

Montreal! What a contrast does this magnificent city of churches, for such it seems to be, afford to the poverty of the country by which it is reached from the East! It is a most delightful surprise. No city on the continent, not even beautiful Minneapolis, is more picturesque in its situation. It is locked in the arms of the St. Lawrence and the Ottawa, and Mount Royal in its green robes bends over it as if with fatherly care. On one hand foam the rapids; on the other solitary mountains rise into strange blue skies, and amid all this beauty the city lifts her spires in dignified repose, a monumental splendor.

Those who have read Moore's American poetry associate this part of Canada with the romance of old days. Among the stories that Gentleman Jo related to the Class on approaching Montreal was one which he called: —

TOM MOORE IN AMERICA.

In 1803 Thomas Moore, then twenty-four years of age, received the appointment of the office of Registrar in the Admiralty Court of Bermuda. He had published two volumes of poems, had won a high reputation in the social circles of London as a singer and pianist, and his heart was full of romance. Life looked to him like a summer day. He visited Bermuda soon after his appointment, but the island of blue skies and perpetual summer had no charms for him like the social circles of London, and he arranged with a deputy to do his work, and soon returned to the world's metropolis.

On his journey home, he visited the United States and Canada, and was inspired by the picturesque scenery to compose some of his most beautiful ballads.

He visited Boston in the spring of 1804, and proceeded to New York; thence he sailed to Norfolk, Virginia. The landscape of America, clothed in the fresh beauty of early summer-time, was a perpetual delight to him; but American society, which at this time had a tendency to be rude, curious, and boastful, constantly disappointed him.

"The Lake of the Dismal Swamp," to which Covert, the author of the "Sword of Bunker Hill," wrote such romantic ballad music, was suggested to Moore while at Norfolk. He wrote it in that place. He had been told the story of a young man who lost his reason on account of the death of a girl he loved. In his madness, the lover thought she had gone to the lake of the Dismal Swamp. He disappeared, and it was believed that he had gone into the swamp in search of his loved one, and had there perished:—

"They made her a grave, too cold and damp
For a soul so warm and true;
And she's gone to the Lake of the Dismal Swamp,
Where, all night long, by a fire-fly lamp,
She paddles her white canoe."

Philadelphia pleased Moore. On leaving it he wrote a ballad rarely equalled in beauty, beginning, —

"Alone by the Schuylkill a wanderer roved."

He visited Niagara Falls, passed through Canada, and returned to England by the way of the St. Lawrence to the ocean. It was during this last tour that he was led to write the ballad presenting an exquisite picture of Arcadian happiness beginning, —

YOUNG MEN'S CHRISTIAN ASSOCIATION, MONTREAL.

"I knew by the smoke that so gracefully curled."

Nothing that Moore wrote in America has had so great and enduring popularity as his "Canadian Boat Song." He wrote it on the Ottawa.

The *voyageurs*, he says, had good voices, and sang perfectly in tune together. The original words of the air, to which he adapted these stanzas, appeared to be a long, incoherent story, of which he could understand but little, from the peculiar pronunciation of the Canadians. It begins, —

Dans mon chemin j'ai rencontré
Deux cavaliers tres-bien montés ;

And the refrain to every verse was, —

A l'ombre d'un bois je m'en vais jouer,
A l'ombre d'un bois je m'en vais danser.

He ventured to harmonize this air, and published it. Without that charm which association gives to every little memorial of scenes or feelings that are past, the melody may, perhaps, be thought common and trifling ; but he says he remembers when he had entered, at sunset, upon one of those beautiful lakes into which the St. Lawrence so grandly and unexpectedly opens, that he had

POST OFFICE, MONTREAL.

heard this simple air with a pleasure which the compositions of the finest masters have never given him.

"Faintly as tolls the evening chime
Our voices keep tune and our oars keep time,
Soon as the woods on shore look dim,
We'll sing at St. Ann's our parting hymn.
Row, brothers, row, the stream runs fast,
The Rapids are near, and the daylight's past.

"Why should we yet our sail unfurl?
There is not a breath the blue wave to curl;
But when the wind blows off the shore,
Oh! sweetly we'll rest our weary oar.
Blow, breezes, blow, the stream runs fast,
The Rapids are near, and the daylight's past.

."Utawas' tide! this trembling moon
Shall see us float over thy surges soon.

Saint of this green isle ! hear our prayers,
Oh, grant us cool heavens and favoring airs.
Blow, breezes, blow, the stream runs fast,
The Rapids are near, and the daylight's past."

ROW, BROTHERS, ROW.

He had been reading Priestley's "Lectures on History." On the fly-leaf of this volume he penned the Canadian air, thus : —

On the same leaf he wrote the first stanza of the song, and the music to the words which the original air suggested. "In my own setting of the air," he says, "I departed in almost every respect but the time from the strain our *voyageurs* had sung to us, leaving the music of the glee as much my own as the words."

The romance of early Canadian life and scenery is embodied in these words and music. The traveller to Montreal approaches the city with this song ever in mind. As he looks down from Mount Royal on the lovely city locked in the arms of the river, and sees the rapids foaming a little above the calm waters

NIAGARA.

that flow before him, this song rings in his ears. He hears it at evening, as the shadows fall on the villas, orchards, and woods:—

"Row, brothers, row; the stream runs fast,
The Rapids are near, and the daylight's past."

The boys visited the French Cathedral, ascended one of its towers, and were charmed with the striking of its melodious bell; the Jesuits' church, and were filled with wonder at its frescos; the English Cathedral, and were as much surprised at its impressive beauty. The same day found them on the St. Lawrence on their way to Niagara Falls through the Thousand Islands.

THE FRENCH CATHEDRAL.

We leave the artist to describe the beauty, majesty, and grandeur of Niagara, as far as pencil can convey an impression of the stupendous waterfall. The Niagara River is only thirty-three miles long, and in this short distance makes a descent of three hundred and thirty-four feet. Through this small channel are poured the waters of the four great Upper Lakes or fresh inland seas on their way to the St. Lawrence.

The Class went to Cleveland by rail, along the shore of the most charming of the inland seas, Lake Erie.

Cleveland, called the Forest City, is beautifully situated on the shore of the lake, and is laid out in squares. It might be named the Maple City, from the maple-trees that everywhere in summer cast a cooling shade. It is one of the most lovely cities of the Middle States, and Euclid Avenue, with its elegant residences and bowery lawns, is regarded as the most picturesque street in the country.

The Class visited the statue of Commodore Perry, the hero of Lake Erie, in the Park, and then was driven to the Lake View Cemetery on the heights, some miles from the city. Here is the temporary tomb of President Garfield; and here, in a lot overlooking the city and the lake, his monument is to be erected, and his tomb to become the American citizens' shrine.

GARFIELD PRESENTING HIMSELF AT HIRAM COLLEGE.

It was a bright midsummer day; the air was cooled by the lake winds; below was the busy city lifting her spires like fingers of faith through the trees; afar, the blue lake stretched away and seemed to meet the sky, which, in the distance, appeared like a canopy of purple with glimmering fringes. White sails like sea-birds flitted hither and thither on the lake, and, amid all, a holy and majestic memory lent to the varying scenes of nature an historic association that completed the charm.

"Step by step," said Master Lewis, as he stood before the President's tomb, "Step by step, and each step in the right direction, leading to a higher one, and after a time to those levels which few men reach, until at last he stood solitary in the highest place of all.

"In life's first years a hard-working orphan boy. In youth a canal

STATUE OF COMMODORE PERRY.

boy, running over a tow-path. At eighteen studying to repair the defects of his early education. A teacher in a country school, making, by his own exertions, a preparation for college. A collegian, living in the most simple and inexpensive manner, and paying his own bills. A graduate from Williams College, receiving the highest honors of his class. A college professor. Before the age of thirty a member of the Ohio Legislature. A colonel. A brigadier-general. Made a major-general for heroic conduct on the battle-field. A member of the National House of Representatives. A senator in the National Senate. President of the United States. A departed statesman, whose lessons of life will be an eternal influence."

He added: "'Character is everything,' said Charles Sumner on his death-bed. The lesson of all this wonderful biography is just *that:* Garfield had character and a positive religious faith, and in each are the laws that govern success. Poverty cannot hinder such a youth from becoming a noble man. It is the soul that makes a man royal; and the jewels that crown a man a king come not from outward mines, but from what he is and aspires to be.

JAMES ABRAM GARFIELD.

"'Howe'er it be, it seems to me
'T is only noble to be good;
Kind hearts are more than coronets,
And simple faith than Norman blood.'"

"We hoped to visit the tombs of three great Presidents on our journey," said Gentleman Jo, — "Garfield's, Lincoln's, and Washington's. Lake View Cemetery is indeed a worthy place for the tomb of a statesman. Garfield rests by the lake, Lincoln on the prairie, and Washington by the Potomac. The scene of the tomb of each is in harmony with the life of each, as much so as the splendid tombs in the Escurial, and the English and French cathedrals are in keeping with the lives of kings. A simple and beautiful rural scene is the fitting place for the tomb of a hero and statesman of a republic like ours. I am glad I can stand by Garfield's grave in the open, free air."

GARFIELD.

Fair inland sea, whose bowery shores
   Arrest the feet that roam,
That stretches far thy crystal floors
   'Neath heaven's golden dome!
Of all the prairie seas most fair,
   Fame lifts above thy deeps
Her latest shaft of honor where
   Her latest hero sleeps.

Peace smiles upon the hills and dells,
   Peace smiles upon the seas ;
And drop the notes of happy bells
   Upon the fruited trees.
The broad Missouri stretches far
   Her commerce-gathering arms,
And multiply on Arkansas
   The grain-encumbered farms.

Old Chattanooga, crowned with green,
   Sleeps 'neath her walls in peace ;
The Argo has returned again,
   And brings the Golden Fleece.
O nation ! free from sea to sea,
   In union blessed forever,
Fair be their fame who fought for thee
   By Chickamauga River.

The autumn winds were piping low
   Beneath the vineclad eaves ;
We heard the hollow bugle blow
   Among the ripened sheaves.

And fast the mustering squadrons passed
  Through mountain portals wide,
And swift the blue brigades were massed
  By Chickamauga's tide.

It was the Sabbath, and in awe
  We heard the dark hills shake,
And o'er the mountain turrets saw
  The smoke of battle break.
And, 'neath that war-cloud, gray and grand,
  The hills o'erhanging low,
The Army of the Cumberland,
  Unequal, met the foe!

Again, O fair September night!
  Beneath the moon and stars,
I see, through memories dark and bright,
  The altar fires of Mars.
The morning breaks with screaming guns
  From batteries dark and dire,
And where the Chickamauga runs,
  Red runs the muskets' fire.

I see bold Longstreet's darkening host
  Sweep through our lines of flame,
And hear again, "The right is lost!"
  Swart Rosecrans exclaim.
"But not the left," young Garfield cries;
  "From that we must not sever,
While Thomas holds the field that lies
  On Chickamauga River!"

Oh, on that day of clouded gold,
  How, half of hope bereft,
The cannoneers, like Titans, rolled
  Their thunders on the left!
I see the battle-clouds again,
  With glowing autumn splendors blending.
It seemed as if the gods with men
  Were on Olympian heights contending.

Through tongues of flame, through meadows brown,
  Dry valley roads concealed,
Ohio's hero dashes down
  Upon the rebel field.

And swift, on reeling charger borne,
　　He threads the wooded plain,
By twice an hundred cannon mown,
　　And reddened with the slain.

But past the swathes of carnage dire,
　　The Union guns he hears,
And gains the left, begirt with fire,
　　And thus the heroes cheers, —
"While stands the left, yon flag o'erhead,
　　Shall Chattanooga stand!"
"Let the Napoleons rain their lead!"
　　Was Thomas's command.

Back swept the gray brigades of Bragg,
　　The air with victory rung,
And Wurzel's "Rally round the flag!"
　　'Mid Union cheers was sung.
The flag on Chattanooga's height
　　In twilight's crimson waved,
And all the clustered stars of white
　　Were to the Union saved.

O chief of staff, the nation's fate
　　That red field crossed with thee,
The triumph of the camp and State,
　　The hope of liberty!
O nation, free from sea to sea,
　　With union blessed forever,
Not vainly heroes fought for thee
　　By Chickamauga River!

In dreams I stand beside the tide;
　　Where those old heroes fell,
Above the valleys, long and wide,
　　Sweet rings the Sabbath bell.
I hear no more the bugle blow,
　　As on that fateful day:
I hear the ring-dove fluting low,
　　Where shaded waters stray.

On Mission Ridge the sunlight streams
　　Above the fields of fall,
And Chattanooga calmly dreams
　　Beneath her mountain wall.

ASSASSINATION OF GARFIELD.

A STORY-TELLING JOURNEY. 141

. Old Lookout Mountain towers on high,
  As in heroic days,
When 'neath the battle in the sky
  Were seen its summit's blaze.

'T was ours to lay no garlands fair
  Upon the graves "unknown."
Kind nature sets her gentians there
  And fall the sere leaves lone.
Those heroes' graves no shaft of Mars
  May mark with beauty ever,
But floats the flag of forty stars
  By Chickamauga River.

From Cleveland the Class semi-circled the lake, and next rested at the old historic city of Detroit,

CHAPTER VI.

THE STORY OF DETROIT.

Pontiac's Conspiracy. — The Romantic Voyage of Marquette.

HE early history of Detroit is highly romantic. It was founded in 1701 by La Motte-Cadillac, who brought hither a small military colony. It soon became one of the most important of the western outposts of Canada, and as the French and Indians were usually on the most friendly terms, the colony here for a long time existed in a state of truly Arcadian happiness. At the close of the French war Detroit contained over two thousand inhabitants. The banks of the river for miles were lined with picturesque Canadian dwellings and lovely gardens. Within the limits of the settlement were several Indian villages. Here the light-hearted French Canadian smoked his pipe and told his story, and the friendly Indian supplied him with game and joined in his merry-making.

In the year 1760 Detroit was taken possession of by the British. The Indians hated the British as greatly as they had loved the French.

Pontiac was the ruling spirit of the forests at this time, a most powerful and statesman-like chief. When he found that his friends

MERRY-MAKING.

the French had lost their power, he sought to unite the Indian tribes against the English colonies, and to destroy the English garrison at Detroit by strategy. He was chief of the Ottawas, but possessed great

GLADWYN AND THE INDIAN GIRL.

influence over other tribes, especially the Ojibwas and the Pottawattamies. Pontiac believed, and that truly, that the establishment of English colonies would be fatal to the interests of the Indian race.

He strode through the forests like a giant, inciting the tribes to war. He urged a union of all the Indian nations from the Lakes to the Mississippi for the common defence of the race.

There lived near Detroit a beautiful Ojibwa girl called Catharine. The English commander, Gladwyn, was pleased with her and bestowed upon her favors, and she formed a warm attachment for him.

One lovely day in May this girl came to the fort and brought Gladwyn a pair of elk-skin moccasons. She appeared very sad.

"Catharine," said Gladwyn, "what troubles you to-day?"

She did not answer at once. There was a silent struggle going on in her heart. She loved Gladwyn, and she also was devoted to her race.

"To-morrow," she said at length, "Pontiac will come to the fort with sixty of his chiefs. Each will be armed with a gun, cut short and hidden under his blanket. The chief will ask to hold a council. He will then make a speech, and offer a belt of wampum as a peace offering. As soon as he holds up the belt, the chiefs will spring up and shoot the officers, and the Indians outside will fall upon the English. Every Englishman will be killed. The French inhabitants will be spared."

Gladwyn made immediate preparation for the emergency. The men were put under arms.

The next morning Indian canoes approached the fort from the eastern shores. They contained Pontiac and his sixty chiefs. At ten o'clock the chiefs marched to the fort, a fantastic procession. Each wore a colored blanket, and was painted, plumed, or in some way gayly ornamented.

As Pontiac entered the fort, a glance showed him that his plot was discovered. He passed in amazement through rows of glittering steel. He made a speech, expressing friendship, but he did not dare to lift the wampum belt, which was to have been the signal for attack. He was allowed to depart peaceably. Foiled in his plot, his anger knew no bounds. He gathered his warriors from every hand and laid siege to Detroit.

EARLY EMIGRANTS AND THEIR CAPTORS.

He was defeated, and with his defeat ended the power of the Indian tribes in the region of the Upper Lakes. Detroit became an English town, an American city, and gathered to herself the wealth of the fertile regions around her, and the commerce of the broad inland seas on either hand. She has to-day more than one hundred and twenty thousand inhabitants, and is famous for her wealth, culture, and benevolence.

The Class spent a few hours in Detroit, walked through the broad, shaded avenues that radiate from the Grand Circus as from a common centre, admired the fine parks, noble churches, and splendid stores. Then Westward again, towards Chicago, a short, bright journey, through towns of wonderful beauty, thrift, growth, and enterprise.

"Marquette with all his visions never dreamed of a scene like this when he crossed Michigan," said Gentleman Jo. " Let me tell you a story, which you have read already in verse. You will do well to keep it in mind amid the surprises of Chicago and the scenes of energy and wealth that you will everywhere meet in Illinois. I have recalled it a thousand times in the West, because it suggests to my mind the contrasts of two hundred years."

HOW MARQUETTE WAS RECEIVED BY THE ILLINOIS.

A little more than two hundred years ago Louis Joliet, a French Jesuit priest who had turned fur-trader, set out from Canada on an expedition to discover the Mississippi.

He took with him Jacques Marquette, a Jesuit, born in 1637 of an old and honorable family at Laon, in the North of France. In 1666 Marquette was sent to Canada to engage in missionary work, chiefly among the Indians. He was full of zeal for his church, and went into the forest sanctuaries with a heart burning for the conversion of the Indian tribes along the shores of the great inland seas.

Marquette was a highly poetic as well as a religious man. He was a devout votary of the Virgin Mary, whom he pictured to himself and others as a being who united in herself all forms of transcendent loveliness. "A subtile element of romance," says Parkman, "was blended with the fervor of his worship, and hung like an illumined cloud over the harsh and hard realities of his daily lot. Kindled by the smile of his celestial mistress, his gentle and noble nature knew no fear."

The outfit for this expedition consisted of two birch canoes and a supply of baked meat and Indian corn. The two adventurers started May 17, 1673, taking with them five men.

It will be interesting for you to run your eye over the map in this old history and to trace the course of this simple but wonderful expedition that opened the West to the knowledge of the world.

Passing from the point where branch the three Great Lakes, the adventurers entered Lake Michigan by the Straits of Michilimackinac, and thence went to Green Bay. Their course was then to Lake Winnebago by the way of the Fox River, past landscapes made beautiful with luxuriant growths of wild rice over which the atmosphere glimmered with the wings of countless birds. On June 17 they reached the lands of the Mascontins and Miamis. (See map.)

They carried their canoes from the Fox River to the Wisconsin, over a long prairie marsh, thus leaving behind the water courses of the St. Lawrence. Over this bridge, whose crossing is a theme worthy of a poet, Marquette and Joliet, in that bright June day, linked two empires; and the greater of these empires was that to which they were going.

Launched on the Wisconsin, the water roads were open to them to the Mississippi, though the voyagers were uncertain as to where the pleasant waters would lead them. They glided down the stream " by islands choked with trees and matted with entangling grape-vines, by forests, groves, and prairies ; under the shadowing trees, between whose tops from afar looked down the bold brow of some woody bluff," says Parkman. They entered at last the eddies of the Upper Mississippi, and then followed the river down into the wonderful realms of midsummer loveliness, of surprise and mystery.

" I cannot express my joy," said Marquette, as he saw the Mississippi. His exultation increased as he drifted down the tide. There was unequalled poetry and romance in this midsummer voyage. Day after day, week after week, the voyagers paddled on.

And now they came to the prairie lands of the Illini, or the Illinois. On the 25th of June, 1673, they discovered footprints on the shore, and they left their canoes and followed them.

They were thus led to an Indian village on the banks of a river, and near by they saw other Indian settlements. One of these villages was called Peoria. (Peonaria).

LA SALLE CLAIMS THE MISSISSIPPI FOR FRANCE.

It was a sunny day. They were unseen by the Indians. Marquette stopped to pray; then they stood forth in plain view of the village and shouted.

There was great excitement in the villages. Presently four of the chief

men came out to meet them, holding up toward the sun peace pipes decorated with feathers.

"What nation are you?" asked Marquette.

"We are the Illinois."

They handed the priest the pipe of peace, and led him to the village.

Here followed a scene which has been beautifully told in verse, but even poetry can hardly exceed the simple facts of Marquette's own narrative.

The chief stood in the door of his wigwam, holding his hands aloft, as a shield from the sun.

"Frenchmen," he said, "how bright the sun shines! It is a good omen; enter our wigwams in peace."

> By the shore of Gitche Gumee,
> By the shining Big-Sea-Water,
> At the doorway of his wigwam,
> In the pleasant summer morning,
> Hiawatha stood and waited.
> . . . . .
> And the noble Hiawatha,
> With his hands aloft extended,

Held aloft in sign of welcome,
Waited, full of exultation,
Till the birch canoe with paddles
Grated on the shining pebbles,
Stranded on the sandy margin,
Till the Black-Robe chief, the Pale-face,
With the cross upon his bosom,
Landed on the sandy margin.

Then the joyous Hiawatha
Cried aloud and spake in this wise ;
" Beautiful is the sun, O strangers,
When you come so far to see us !
All our town in peace awaits you,
All our doors stand open for you ;
You shall enter all our wigwams,
For the heart's right hand we give you.

" Never bloomed the earth so gayly,
Never shone the sun so brightly,
As to-day they shine and blossom
When you come so far to see us!
Never was our lake so tranquil,
Nor so free from rocks and sand-bars ;
For your birch canoe in passing
Has removed both rock and sand-bar.

" Never before had our tobacco
Such a sweet and pleasant flavor,
Never the broad leaves of our cornfields
Were so beautiful to look on,
As they seem to us this morning,
When you come so far to see us ! "

And the Black-Robe chief made answer,
Stammered in his speech a little,
Speaking words yet unfamiliar :
" Peace be with you, Hiawatha,
Peace be with you and your people,
Peace of prayer, and peace of pardon,
Peace of Christ, and joy of Mary ! "

Then the generous Hiawatha
Led the strangers to his wigwam,
Seated them on skins of bison,
Seated them on skins of ermine,
And the careful old Nokomis
Brought them food in bowls of bass-wood,
Water brought in birchen dippers,
And the calumet, the peace-pipe,
Filled and lighted for their smoking.

FIRST WHITE MEN ON THE "GREAT RIVER."

The voyagers were taken by the chief men who first welcomed them to the great chief of the Illinois, who made a feast for them. The scene was much like that described in "Hiawatha;" it was worthy of the poet and presents a noble subject to the painter.

Marquette and Joliet descended the river as far as the Arkansas, then returned to Green Bay in the beautiful September days, having travelled twenty-five hundred miles.

A wasting disease had set its mark on the Jesuit father, and for years he

DEATH OF MARQUETTE.

struggled against it. He had promised the Indians of Kaskaskia, a town of the Illinois, that he would return to them and preach to them the mysteries of God. He never forgot the promise.

He returned. We are told he was received "like an angel from heaven." His body was wasted; he had stopped on his way to pray for strength, at one place continuing in prayer nine days.

It was his last mission. "He passed," says the historian, "from wigwam to wigwam, telling the listening crowds of God and the Virgin, Paradise and Hell, angels and demons, and when he thought their minds prepared, he summoned them to a grand council."

This took place near the modern town of Utica. Five hundred chiefs were present, seated in a ring. The dying Jesuit preached to them the Gospel with fiery ardor and self-consuming zeal.

He left the village just after Easter (1675) escorted by a large company of Indians, who followed him to Lake Michigan. Thence he set sail for Michilimackinac.

It was his last voyage. He lay in the canoe in a dying state communing with God and with angels. The canoe passed near the mouth of a small river.

"Let us land here," he said to his companions.

They carried him to the shore, and made for him a shed of bark.

"I thank God I am permitted to die in the wilderness a missionary of the Faith."

Night came.

"Take your rest," he said; "I will call you when I find my time approaching."

Near midnight they heard a feeble call.

"Jesu — Mary."

They buried him near the river which now bears his name.

In the spring of 1676 the Ottawas visited the grave of their spiritual father. They removed the body, washed and dried the bones, and, in a procession of thirty canoes, bore them over the lake to Michilimackinac. There the relics were received with funeral songs and solemn ceremonies, and buried beneath the floor of the little chapel of the Jesuit mission.

JESUIT FATHERS.

CHAPTER VII.

THE STORY OF CHICAGO.

THE FRENCH MISSIONARIES. — SIGNING THE TREATY. — THE EMIGRANTS. — LINCOLN'S MONUMENT.

HE Illini were numerous Indian tribes who roamed over the prairies where now is the opulent State to which they have left only their name. Their chiefs were called Cheecaquas; and from these lords of the prairies, long vanished and almost forgotten, it is supposed that the early French settlers on Lake Michigan called their fort Cheecaqua, and so left the name Chicago to the queen city of the West, the mid-ocean metropolis of the United States.

The French missionaries, Marquette and Joliet, and the explorers, Hennepin and La Salle, visited this favorite seat of the Illini on Lake Michigan, and thus the town first became known to the civilized world about the years 1673-74. The French fort was abandoned to Great Britain when Canada was ceded to that country.

In 1831 the old town contained twelve families. It began to grow with the moving of emigration to the fertile lands of the setting sun.

THE TREATY.

The town of Chicago was formally organized Aug. 10, 1833. It then contained five hundred and fifty inhabitants.

On Aug. 10, 1883, Chicago may be said to be fifty years old. What a transformation! A half-century will have used the multiplier of one thousand. Chicago to-day numbers more than five hundred thousand inhabitants. She is much larger than Boston, and ere another half-century may be more populous than New York.

That was an eventful day in 1833, when seven thousand Potta-wattamies assembled at Chicago in council and signed a treaty to remove beyond the Mississippi. By this treaty the old tribes ceded

UNION DEPOT.

twenty million acres to the United States. It was September. The chiefs, in a long procession, turned away from the lands of their fathers, and prepared to cross that river that to them had been the golden border of the sunset world. The vanguard of the great army of immigration was already there to see the disappearing plumes. They crossed the Mississippi, and Chicago as it were leaped into the vacant throne, and called to her fertile fields the enterprise of the world.

Her growth was a wonder, and the wonder grew. In 1871 the city was the scene of one of the most destructive fires of modern times. More than two thousand acres of houses were burned, and nearly one hundred thousand persons were rendered homeless.

She brushed the ashes from her garments and rose again. She built merchant palaces where before had been shops, and piled with marble the streets where wooden houses had vanished into smoke. Her public buildings, her parks, her piers and breakwaters assumed colossal proportions. She opened her avenues of prosperity to the East and the West, and made herself the railway centre of America. Her vessels trade on three thousand miles of coast line on the Lakes; by the Welland Canal, between Lakes Erie and Ontario, they visit Montreal and Quebec, and so communicate with the steamers for Europe. She made herself the storehouse and exchange of all the growing industries of the Western Empire, and graced every principal street with stately temples and noble schools.

What if La Salle could have seen the vision of the Chicago of to-day! What if the departing Indian chiefs could have beheld the Illinois of 1883! What if we to-day could behold the city of the prairies of seventeen years from to-day — 1900!

The Class took rooms at the Palmer House, a hotel that in any age of the world might have been regarded as a palace. It is a favorite resort of busy people who stop transiently in the city, and Gentleman Jo chose it for the Class in preference to one of the more quiet and home-like hotels, several of which are stately palaces, because there the coming and going of crowds of business men illustrate the genius and enterprise of the West.

"One can sit in one of the open balconies overlooking the office of the Palmer House," he said, "and see at a glance what the West is and is to be. It is like a play. From early morning until midnight a procession rushes through it like a tide. Every train that enters the city — and is there a minute in the day that a train does not enter the city? — reinforces it. The men come from all the States,

TOWER OF WATER-WORKS.

from all countries. All are in a hurry. Above the sound of tripping feet is heard the bustle of baggage, and the constant announcement of departing trains. The office, which is like an Eastern court, is surrounded with pictures of the history of Chicago. The dining-

PALMER HOUSE, CHICAGO.

rooms are most elegant, fit for the banqueting halls of a king, and there again one may see busy people from every State. All seem bent on one object,— the making of money. Money, money,— all the talk is money. One wonders if these people ever think of God, of the golden rule, of immortality. It is a buzz of speculation everywhere; lands, stocks, railroads. I have sometimes asked, Do these people ever die? To see these surging crowds, with their eager faces, evident wealth, baggage, jewels, one would suppose that death were banished from the world. It is an illusion, a mirage of business, but there beat the pulses of the East and West, and you will there get a view of the nation's enterprises and activities as nowhere else in the West."

The Class visited the noble public buildings, the parks and the stock-yards, and made a short excursion on Lake Michigan.

"We will have to deviate somewhat from the original plan of our journey," said Gentleman Jo to the Class, "and visit Springfield and the tomb of Lincoln from Chicago now, instead of from St. Louis on our return. We may not return by the way of Springfield."

One lovely midsummer morning, while the mist from Lake Michigan still hung like a thin veil over the city, the Class walked to the Union Depot to take the train for Springfield, there to visit the monument to Abraham Lincoln. The depot was a wonderful structure, a surprise, like everything in the West. It is said to be one of the longest in the world.

The Class was early for the train. The boys walked to and fro in the waiting-rooms.

The balconies were full of weary-looking men, and the waiting-rooms as crowded with anxious-looking women. They were all poorly clad, but they had honest, wishful faces. They were not Americans. Finely dressed people brushed by them, and did not seem to notice them.

"Who are these people?" asked Wyllys Wynn of Gentleman Jo.

"Emigrants."

Wyllys passed through the ladies' room, and as he noticed these strange people more closely his heart was touched at their condition. There were mothers with young children in their arms; grandmothers, with wrinkles in their faces, helping their daughters in the care of the children. They all looked weary. Many of them were lunching on simple food.

"I would like to buy some oranges and distribute them among these children," said Wyllys to Gentleman Jo.

THE LITTLE FACES SEEMED TO BLOSSOM WITH DELIGHT.

"You could not do a kinder thing; I will buy some sandwiches and cake, and offer a lunch to the old people."

Wyllys bought the oranges, and hurried back to the room, and offered them to the children. The little ones were eager to receive them, but their mothers forbade it, shaking their heads, and saying, —

"Nein."

Then Gentleman Jo said, —

"Wir gaben sie Ihr."

What a ripple of sunshine passed over all those clouded and

CHAMBER OF COMMERCE.

anxious faces! What warm feelings moistened the eyes! What sudden lightness of heart brought smiles to the lips! The little faces seemed to blossom with delight.

Wyllys distributed the oranges, and received "God-bless-yous" for every gift.

"Why do not churches, benevolent societies, people who wish to do real good, give their sympathy to these deserving people on their way to their new homes?" asked Wyllys.

"I hardly know," said Gentleman Jo.

"I can tell you," said Tommy Toby.

"Why?"

"There are a good many people in the world this year."

"Selfish ones?" asked Wyllys.

The journey was through a country loaded with the riches of the harvest. What cornfields, what wheat-fields, what evidences of thrift, what boundless prosperity!

The city of Springfield seems like a New England country town. The streets really look *old*, a strange thing in the West.

The Class visited the State House. It was a pile of magnificence, half completed inside, — a mountain of unfinished halls, indicating a lavish expenditure of money on one hand, and a strange penuriousness on the other.

"Why did they build the State House on this low land?" asked Wyllys. "Why did they not put such a structure on an elevation, commanding an extended view?"

"Speculation, I have no doubt," said Gentleman Jo.

"Land is scarce in Illinois," said Tommy. "Too many immigrants."

Gentleman Jo asked one of the State officers in the building why these noble halls and offices remained unfinished.

"We are waiting for an appropriation."

The building had evidently been constructed by different legislatures, some of which were disposed to be as liberal as the genius of the West, and others as economical as a New England town council. At least so it looked.

The Lincoln monument is a shrine. People go hundreds, sometimes thousands, of miles to visit it. Every year the number of visitors increases. It must grow in the love and admiration of the nation as the nation itself makes progress and fulfils its destiny. The hand that in the dark days of the war wrote the Emancipation Proclamation conferred a blessing upon every American and upon all who shall share the nation's prosperity. The theories of the Declaration of Independence, the policy of Abraham Lincoln, through the amendments to the Constitution, made realities. His influence gave to man his birthright, and made all men equal before the law.

The monument was paid for by the people, and cost some two hundred thousand dollars. It was begun in 1869, and the statue of Lincoln was placed in position in 1874. It is surmounted by noble groups of statuary of orange-colored bronze, representing the defenders of the nation.

An iron stairway leads to the top of the obelisk, which is one hundred feet high.

The view from the top is delightful. The thrifty city of Springfield, with the majestic dome of the State House rising above it, is two miles away. Rolling prairie lands, filled with immense cornfields and dark groves of oak, present an extended view; and lines of railroads wind away conveying the wealth of these sunny fields to feed the people.

In the base of the monument is Memorial Hall, containing the parchments by which the great cities of the world expressed to Mrs. Lincoln their sympathy and condolence after the assassination. Here is the famous stone from the wall of Servius Tullius, and a piece of the dress of Laura Keene, stained with the President's blood.

The coffin is shown to visitors, who are admitted to the crypt. It is so heavy that it could not be stolen. It consists of a cedar coffin enclosed in lead, which is also enclosed in a marble sarcophagus. The custodian is John Carrol Power, who is the leader of a

THE LINCOLN MONUMENT.

society in Springfield that seeks to keep active the observance of Lincoln memorial days.

The old pioneers of Springfield love to be interviewed on the subject of Lincoln's character, elevation, and influence. Gentleman Jo approached one of them cautiously with the question, —

'Will you tell which was the depot where President Lincoln made his farewell speech to the citizens of Springfield?'"

ORIGINAL STORIES OF LINCOLN.

"God bless every one who loved Abraham Lincoln," were the exact words of this old man, who saw that Gentleman Jo was seeking information out of regard for the hero he had loved; and he gave him, as though it had been a story, a very detailed account of the scene of that memorable speech from the car-platform, in which the departing President asked his neighbors' prayers.

"After Lincoln studied law," said he, "a land agent brought a writ against me, claiming I had not a legal title to my lands. I did not know much about law and was greatly moved; so, you see, I needed honest advice, and I went to Lincoln. 'Don't trouble yourself, Isaac,' he said, 'your papers are all correct. I will attend to the matter before it is brought into court.' The court was held in another part of the district. Lincoln said nothing to me when he met me, and I wondered what had become of my case; at last I said to him, —

"'How about that suit, Lincoln?'

"'Isaac, you will never hear from that again. I have made everything all right. Your title is secure.'

"'But how much am I to pay you for your trouble?'

"'Well, Isaac, about ten dollars.'

"*That* was the kind of man Abraham Lincoln was."

He emphasized the point of his story with a gesture. Lincoln had avoided speaking of the case to him lest his old neighbor should think' he was thereby indirectly seeking the payment for his services; and, when, to save the man's pride, he was obliged to accept compensation, charged him ten dollars!

"Just think of it," continued the man, — "ten dollars! Now I am going to tell you just what I did. When I heard that Abraham Lincoln was nominated for the Presidency, I let the business at my store go for three months, and gave all my time to try to secure his election. I brought here fourteen hundred Wide-Awake suits, organized Lincoln Clubs, and worked for him as I never did for any man." The spirit that Lincoln showed in the ten-dollar fee for securing the suppression of a troublesome case made that man a power in a canvass in which his influence had no money value.

Gentleman Jo had known Mr. Ross, an old citizen of Springfield, and he made him a visit and gave the Class an opportunity to listen to some delightful incidents of the life of the great emancipationist.

"I helped Lincoln build the first flat-boat ever made in Springfield," said Mr. Ross. "It would have made you laugh to have seen him then. He worked for fifteen dollars per month. He used to wear a big hat and blue jean pantaloons. He was very tall, — over six feet high, — and his pantaloons were generally too short, and he strapped them to his brogans to keep them down.

"I knew there was something, in him even then. Why, let me tell you, —

"When Lincoln first came to Salem, he used to walk twenty miles to borrow law books to read. Stewart and Everett were lawyers here then. Lincoln would come up from Salem to borrow a book, and one might have seen him reading it along the way as he returned. When he got tired he would sit down on a log and rest and study. The lawyers here liked him, and — why, the first thing I knew, Stewart and Everett had taken him into the firm. He never would undertake a case in which he did not believe. He practised no tricks in court. You could not turn him aside from principle — 't was no use. Everybody believed what Abraham Lincoln said was the exact truth, and so he became known as 'Honest Abe.'

"He never spoke ill of any one. How I have heard him abused in the courts and on the political platform! But he would never return it; he never spoke evil of any one.

"He gave me his dog when he went away, and the people here came to think so much of him at last that they used to come to my house just to see his dog."

If ever a man was loved in his own town it was Lincoln. It was not his genius, but his honesty of purpose and his great, good heart that made him what he was to his neighbors, to the public, and to the cause of the slave. It does not seem strange that when a great emancipation was needed to direct national affairs, God, who sees the human heart, should have called him from the prairies to this service, and should have made him one of the imperial

LINCOLN RESTING.

wonder-workers of the world, and crowned him at last as the supreme benefactor of the most prosperous nation beneath the sun.

Mrs. Lincoln lives in Springfield, shattered in body and mind. Robert Lincoln is very popular in the West.

"I do believe," said Mr. Ross to Gentleman Jo, "that Robert will get to be President of the United States. He is just like his father."

THE STATE OF LAKES.

Minnesota may be pictured as the State of lakes. There are said to be more than two thousand lakes in this most beautiful region where the St. Lawrence, with its great inland seas, the Mississippi, the father of waters, and the Red River of the North all have their rise. The sources of these mighty water-courses are so near each other that in times of freshets they are said to mingle; and it is claimed that the Indians used to float their light canoes during such overflows from one to the other of these three rivers.

Minnesota is an Indian word, and is said to mean "cloudy water;"

but if ever there was a region whose lakes were clear as crystal, it is this. The name was, however, applied to the Minnesota River, which may be clouded like the Mississippi. The upper part of the State, with its almost countless lakes, its pineries, and the glorious valley of the Red River of the North, is in summer a natural park and one of the most beautiful in the world. It is called the park region.

The Class left Chicago for St. Paul at evening. The boys rose early in the morning, and went to the platform of the car. What a country! What air that the lungs drank in like water! What fields of wheat on the rolling prairies! There were clover-fields stretching as far as the eye could see, doubtless the second crop. There were pretty towns everywhere.

They were eager to catch the first view of the Mississippi. When the train slowly crossed the river they were delighted with the beauty of the bluffs, the picturesqueness of Fort Snelling, near the junction of the Minnesota and Mississippi, but the river at this point was not majestic. As they passed Fort Snelling, the first settlement and military post of the Territory, Gentleman Jo told them incidents of the Sioux war. The region seemed to grow in beauty, and presently the bluffs of St. Paul rose in view, and the city appeared wearing the morning sunlight like a crown.

CHAPTER VIII.

ST. PAUL.

THE STORY OF THE LITTLE SIOUX'S WARNING.

HERE were cities of old that were built in the form of an amphitheatre, their porticoed terraces open to the sun.

Nature laid the foundations of St. Paul, and made it an amphitheatre, with its terraces open to the sun, and overlooking the wonderful river of the Western World.

It is a city of four terraces, rising above the Mississippi, and conforming to the curve of the river.

Trade has built on the first terrace. The residents chiefly occupy the second and third terraces; the fourth terrace needs only an Acropolis to make the resemblance to a Greek city complete.

St. Paul is the capital of Minnesota. The public buildings are here. It is a city of churches and richly endowed schools. It is one of the healthiest cities in the Union.

The view of the rolling prairies, lakes, and rivers from the highest terrace is noble and magnificent. Some four miles from the city is

Lake Como, where three hundred acres have been secured for a public park.

St. Paul was incorporated as a town in 1849, and as a city in 1854. Its situation and enterprise indicate a remarkable future. Its popu-

LAKE COMO.

lation is sweeping on from fifty thousand towards one hundred thousand. The value of public and private buildings erected during the year 1880 was two million dollars, and yet people came to the city more rapidly than homes could be provided for them. The great increase of population continues, and must do so for years.

Lake Como is one of the most beautiful of the two thousand lakes of Minnesota, and its shores are the city's pleasure grounds. The summer evening rides to it are one of the luxuries of the city. Lake Elmo, twelve miles distant, is also a popular summer resort.

The Class found accommodations at a hotel whose elegances and comforts were a surprise,. and after a night's rest in rooms filled with air that made it a luxury to breathe, visited the Indian museum.

"The morning air is like pure water when one is thirsty," said Master Lewis. "My lungs are not strong, and they seem to drink it in as though they were feverish and thirsty. I would like to remain here a week just to enjoy *breathing*."

The Mississippi lay in view, winding away in the crystal air. The sun filled all things with a strange brightness. The boys were in high spirits, they hardly knew why. Was there something electrical in the air?

"This is a beautiful world," said Gentleman Jo.

"Beautiful!" exclaimed all.

"I would like to live in Minnesota," said Wyllys.

They met an old man on the street, and inquired the way to a public building.

"Are you from the East?" asked the old man.

"Yes."

"God bless you. I wish I could once more look upon Cape Ann and breathe the salt air of the sea."

The travellers looked thoughtful.

"Nevertheless," said Gentleman Jo, "this *is* a beautiful world, and blessings alike are the pure, cool atmosphere of Minnesota and the salt air of the coast."

After a day spent in St. Paul and at Lake Como, the Class rested in the parlor of the hotel. Gentleman Jo there met a lady who had come to the territory from the East in the times of the pioneers. She had seen some of the horrors of the Sioux war, and her recollections of the early history of the State were of thrilling interest to the Class.

Among the stories which she related, the one that afforded the clearest picture of the times of the pioneers was the following: —

THE LITTLE SIOUX'S WARNING.

A STORY OF THE SIOUX WAR.

In the summer of 1862, while we were living in the new State of Minnesota, an experience fell to my lot which I regard as one of the most remarkable that I have ever met.

I was a small girl at the time, my tenth birthday coming in that same month of August in which these extraordinary events occurred, and on the very day — the 18th — on which the terrible Sioux massacres of Minnesota broke out at the Lower Agency, as the station was called, and which soon desolated such a large portion of that fair land with fire and blood.

We lived at Lac Qui Parle, or rather quite close to it, for we were a full mile from the place, where at that time the devoted missionary, Amos Huggins, and his young wife and two children were stationed.

There were only three of us, — father, mother, and myself. We had moved to Minnesota three years before, the prime object of my parents being to improve their health, for both were threatened with consumption. At the same time, they felt a natural eagerness to try their fortunes in a new country, where there always seems to be more cause for encouragement than at home.

The first year father and mother were much benefited, but not long after, father began to fail. I was too young to notice the signs at the time, but I recall them now. I remember how he used to take his chair out front in pleasant weather and sit there during the balmy afternoons, so still, with his eyes looking off at the blue horizon or into the solemn depths of the vast stretch of wilderness, which came down to a point scarce a stone's throw from our door.

He would sit there so long and so quiet, that sometimes I thought he was asleep, and would steal softly up to him; but when I did so, I could notice that his eyes were wide open, though he did not seem to know what was going on around him. Mother used to steal to the door sometimes and peep quietly at him, and then raise her finger and shake her head in a warning way for me not to disturb him, and then her white, sad face would disappear in the door again.

Then again she would sometimes come out and sit down beside father, and taking his hand in hers, they would talk long and earnestly in low tones. I was too young, I repeat, to understand all this at the time, but it was not long afterwards that the truth came to me.

Father was steadily and surely declining in health, and he knew he was

PERILS OF FRONTIER LIFE.

doomed to die; but the same climate which was thus killing one of my parents was healing the other, for mother became strong and robust, and the seeds of the dreadful disease soon left her system altogether.

There is nothing which makes us feel so hopeful as strong, sturdy health; and when mother felt the life-blood bounding through her veins, and her strength increasing, she could not quite fully realize that it was different with father.

She tried to encourage him, and really believed his weakness was only temporary. There were times when he caught a little of her hopefulness, and thought it possible he was going to get well. Consumption, I am sure, is the most deceptive of all ailments in this respect.

But these self-deceptions did not last long. He saw that death had marked him for its own, and a deep melancholy settled over him, which in reality hastened the ravages of the disease. He became touchingly tender and loving to mother and me, and when he was not sitting in front of the house, in his deep, sorrowful reveries, or if the day was stormy, at the window, looking out into vacancy, he was fondling and caressing one of us.

I remember that more than once I saw tears in his eyes, though I could not tell why; for he and mother agreed to keep his fears, or rather his certainty of what was fast coming, from me, and I never once suspected that death was already looking into our window upon us.

Scarcely a day passed that I did not see some of the Indians who were scattered through that section. The Sioux seemed to be everywhere, and in going to and coming from the Agency, they would sometimes stop at our house.

Father was very quick in picking up languages, and he was able to converse quite intelligently with the red men. How I used to laugh to hear them talk in their odd language, which sounded to me, for all the world, just as if they were grunting at each other like so many pigs.

But the visits used to please father and mother, and I was always glad to see some of the rather dilapidated and not over-clean warriors stop at the house to get something to eat and to talk with father.

I recall one hot day in June, when he was sitting under the single tree in front of the house, his chair leaning back, his feet resting on the seat of another, while he was looking away off towards the setting sun, as though striving to pierce the blue depths of space, and to catch just one glimpse of the wonderful world beyond. I was in the house helping mother when we heard the peculiar noises which told us that father had an aboriginal visitor. We both went to the door, and I passed outside to laugh at their queer talk.

Sure enough, an Indian was seated in the other chair, and he and father were talking with great animation.

The Indian was of a stout build, and wore a hat like father's, — the ordinary straw one, — with a broad red band around it ; he had on a fine black broadcloth coat, with silk velvet collar, but his trousers were shabby and his shoes were pretty well worn. His face was bright and intelligent, and I watched it very narrowly as he talked and gesticulated in his earnest way with father, who was equally animated in answering him. Their discussion was of more than ordinary importance.

The Indian carried a rifle and revolver, — the latter being in plain sight at his waist, — but I never connected the thought of danger with him as he sat there in converse with father.

I describe this Indian rather closely, because he was no other than the celebrated chief Little Crow, who was at the head of the frightful Minnesota massacres which broke out within the succeeding sixty days, and who even then was perfecting his plans for one of the most atrocious series of crimes ever perpetrated in our history. Little Crow was a thoroughly bad Indian, who would have accepted food with one hand while he drove the knife into the heart of his friend with the other.

The famous chieftain stayed till the sun went down. Then he suddenly sprang up and walked away at a rapid, shuffling walk in the direction of Lac Qui Parle. Father called good-by to him, but he did not make a reply, and soon disappeared in the woods, through which his path led.

The sky was cloudy, and it looked as if a storm was coming; so, as it was dark and blustering, we remained within doors the rest of the time. There was no thunder or lightning, but a fine drizzling rain began falling, and the darkness was intense. It was really impossible to see anything at all beyond the range of the rays thrown out by the candle burning on the table near the window. The evening was well advanced, and father had opened the Bible, with the purpose of reading a chapter before prayers, as was his rule, when there came a rap upon the door.

It was so gentle and timid that it sounded like the pecking of a bird, and we all looked inquiringly in the direction, uncertain what it meant. The next moment it was repeated, and then it kept on in a way which no person would do who knew anything about knocking.

"It is some bird, scared by the storm," said father, "and we may as well admit it."

I sat much nearer the door than either of my parents, and instantly sprang up and opened it. As I did so, I peered down in the gloom and rain for the bird, but sprang back the next moment with a low cry of alarm.

"What's the matter?" asked father, hastily laying down his Bible and walking rapidly towards me.

"It isn't a bird; it's a person." As I spoke, a little Indian girl, about my

"IT IS N'T A BIRD."

own age, walked into the room, and looking in each of our faces, asked in the Sioux tongue whether she could stay all night.

I had closed the door and we gathered around her. She had the prettiest, daintiest moccasons, though her limbs were bare from the knee downward. She wore a large shawl about her shoulders and down almost to her ankles, while her coarse black hair hung loosely below her waist. Her face was very pretty, and her eyes were as black as coal and seemed to flash fire upon whomsoever she looked. I never beheld a more animated countenance.

Of course, her clothing was dripping with moisture, and her call filled us all with wonder. She could speak only a few words of English, so her face lit up with pleasure when father addressed her in the Sioux tongue ; and straightway a lively conversation began between them.

As near as we could find out her meaning, her name was Chit-to ; and father gathered from her that she lived with her parents at Lac Qui Parle. There were several families in a spot by themselves, and they had begun a carouse that day ; that is, they had supplied themselves plentifully with firewater, and were all drinking at a fearful rate and just the same as if they were white men.

At such times the Indian is dangerous, and these carousals nearly always end in crime and murder. Little Chit-to was terrified almost out of her senses ; and when she saw the knives, tomahawks, and pistols doing their deadly work, she fled through the storm and darkness, not caring where she went, but only anxious to get away from the dreadful scene.

Entering, without any intention on her part, the path in the woods, she followed it until she caught the glimmer of the light in our window, when she hastened to it and asked our hospitality.

I need scarcely say it was gladly granted. My mother removed the damp clothes from the little Sioux girl, and replaced them with some warm, dry ones belonging to me. At the same time, she gave her hot, refreshing tea, and did everything in her power to make her comfortable.

In this Good Samaritan work I did all I could, as was natural in one of my tender years. I removed the little moccasons from the wondering Chit-to's feet, rubbed the latter with my hands to bring back the circulation, kissed her dark cheeks, and while flying about in the aimless manner peculiar to childhood, I was continually uttering expressions of pity which, though in an unknown tongue, I am quite sure were understood by Chit-to, who looked the gratitude she could not express.

When father read the Bible, she listened in her wondering way, and then, as we all knelt and prayed to God, she imitated our movement, though it cannot be supposed that she understood what it meant. Then she began to show signs of drowsiness and was put to bed with me, falling asleep as soon as her head touched the pillow.

I lay awake a little longer and noticed that the storm subsided. The patter of the rain was heard no more upon the roof, and the wind blew just as it sometimes does late in the fall. At last I sank into slumber.

I awoke in the morning and saw the rays of the sun entering the window. Recalling the incidents of the previous evening, I turned over quickly to see and speak to my young friend. To my surprise she was gone, and supposing she had risen a short time before, I hurriedly dressed myself and went down to help keep her company.

But she was not there, and father and mother had seen nothing of her. The investigation that father then made showed that she had no doubt risen in the night and stolen away. Very likely she was afraid of the vengeance of her parents for fleeing, and, as the rainfall had ceased, she hastened back through the woods to their wigwam.

There was something curious and touching in the fact that she had groped about in the darkness, for she could not have used a light, until she found her own clothing, which she donned and departed without taking so much as a pin that belonged to us.

We all felt a strong interest in Chit-to, and I was sensible of something akin to strong friendship. Father allowed me to go with him a few days later when he visited Lac Qui Parle, and he made many inquiries there for the little girl, but he could find out nothing. No one seemed to know to whom we referred, and we went home — especially I did — very much disappointed, for I had built up strong hopes of taking her out with me to spend several days. I was sure that it would n't take us more than a couple of days to learn each other's language. At any rate, we would learn to understand each other in that time.

We went several times after, and neglected no effort to discover Chit-to; but we did not gain the first clew.

On the afternoon of August 19, father was sitting in his accustomed seat in front of the house, and mother was engaged as usual about her household duties, while I was playing and amusing myself as a girl of my age is inclined to do at all times. The day was sultry and close, and I remember that father was unusually pale and weak. He coughed a great deal, and sat a long time so still that I thought he must be asleep.

"Mother," said I, "what is that smoke yonder?"

I pointed in the direction of Lac Qui Parle, the stretch of woods lying between us and the station. She saw a dark column of smoke floating off in the horizon, its location being such that there could be no doubt it was at the Agency.

"There is a fire of some kind there," she said in a low voice, as if speaking to herself, while she shaded her eyes with her hand, and gazed long and earnestly in the direction.

"The Indians are coming, Edward," she called to father; "they will be here in a few minutes!"

As she spoke, she darted into the house and came forth with father's rifle. Knowing how weak he was, she intended to use it herself.

Brief as was the time she was away, it was long enough for a galloping horse to come in view. Suddenly a splendid black steed thundered from the

CHIT-TO.

wood, and, with two or three tremendous bounds, halted directly in front of me. As it did so, I saw that the bareback rider was a small girl, and she was our little Sioux guest, Chit-to.

She made a striking picture, with her long black hair streaming over her shoulders and her scant dress fluttering in the wind. Her attire was the same as when at our house, excepting she had not the cumbersome shawl.

"Why, Chit-to," said I, in amazement, "where did you come from?"

"Must go — must go — must go!" she exclaimed, in great excitement. "Indian soon be here!"

So it seemed that in the few weeks since she had been at our house, she had picked up enough of the English tongue to make herself understood, though it is not impossible that she knew enough when our guest, but chose to conceal it. It is very hard to fathom all the whims and peculiarities of the Indian race.

"What do you mean?" asked mother, as she and I advanced to the side of the black steed upon which the little Sioux sat; "what are the Indians doing?"

"They burn buildings — have killed missionary — coming dis way!"

Chit-to spoke the truth, for the Sioux were raging like demons at that very hour at Lac Qui Parle, and one of their first victims was the good missionary, Amos Huggins, whose wife and children, however, escaped through the friendliness of some of the Sioux.

"What shall we do, Chit-to?"

"Get on horse — he carry you."

"But my husband; the horse cannot carry all three of us."

"He hide in wood."

My poor distracted mother scarcely knew what to do. All this time father sat like a statue in his chair. A terrible suspicion suddenly entered her mind, and she ran to him. Placing her hand upon his shoulder, she addressed him in a low tone, and then gave utterance to a fearful shriek, as she staggered backward.

"O heaven! he is dead!"

Such was the fact. The shock of the news brought by the little Indian girl was too much, and he had expired in his chair without a struggle. Mother would have swooned but for the imminence of the danger. The wild cry which escaped her was answered by several whoops from the woods, and Chit-to became frantic with terror.

"Indian be here in minute!" said she.

Mother instantly helped me upon the back of the horse and then followed herself. She was a skilful equestrian, but she allowed Chit-to to retain the bridle. The horse moved off on a walk, and the whoops were heard again. Looking back I saw a half-dozen Sioux horsemen emerge from the wood and start on a trot toward us, spreading out as if they meant to surround us.

Several shots were fired which must have come close to us, but just then Chit-to gave the horse rein, and he bounded off at a terrible rate, never halting until he had gone two or three miles, by which time I was so jolted that I felt as if I should die with pain.

Then, when we looked back, we saw nothing of the Indians, and the horse was brought down to a walk; and finally, when the sun went down, we drove into a dense wood, where we stayed all night.

I shall not attempt to describe those fearful hours. Not one of us slept a wink. Mother sat crying, moaning, and weeping over the loss of father, while I was heart-broken, too. Chit-to, like the Indian she was, kept on the move continually. Here and there she stole as noiselessly through the wood as a shadow, while playing the part of sentinel.

At daylight we all fell into a feverish slumber, which lasted several hours. When we awoke we were hungry and miserable.

Seeing a settler's house in the distance, Chit-to volunteered to go to it for food. We were afraid she would get into trouble, but she was sure there was none and went.

In less than an hour she was back again with an abundance of bread. She said the house was deserted, the occupants having, no doubt, become terror-stricken; but the Sioux had not visited it as yet.

We stayed where we were for three days, during which we saw a party of Sioux warriors ride up on horseback and burn the house and out-buildings where Chit-to had obtained the food for us.

It seemed to mother that the Indians would not remain at Lac Qui Parle long, and that we would be likely to find safety there. Accordingly, she induced Chit-to to start on the return. Poor soul! she was yearning to learn what had become of father's body. When we reached the house nothing was to be seen of it, but she soon discovered a newly made grave, where she had reason to believe he was buried. As was afterwards ascertained, he had been given a decent burial by orders of Little Crow himself, who doubtless would have been glad to protect us had we awaited his coming.

We rode carefully through the wood, and when we emerged on the opposite side our hearts were made glad by the sight of the white tents of United States soldiers. Colonel Sibley was encamped at Lac Qui Parle, and we were safe at last.

Chit-to disappeared from this post in the same sudden fashion as before; but I am happy to say that I have seen her several times since. Mother and I were afraid her people would punish her for the part she took in befriending us, but they never interfered with her at all. Probably the friendship which Little Crow evinced toward our family may have had something to do with the leniency which they showed her.

EMIGRANTS ON THE MISSOURI.

CHAPTER IX.

MINNEAPOLIS.

" BEAUTIFUL MINNEAPOLIS!"— A STRANGE STORY.

IN 1850 there was no Minneapolis. To-day the city has more than seventy thousand inhabitants; it will soon have a hundred thousand; it is found impossible to build houses sufficient to meet the demands of emigration.

In its situation and surroundings Minneapolis is perhaps the most picturesque inland city in the Union. Socially it is a New England city, — a new Boston in the region of Lakes.

The Falls of St. Anthony, turning the wheels of the flour-mills and saw-mills, flow like a park of fountains through the very centre of the city. The Mississippi divides the city like a water street. From the wonderful bridges over it one delights to gaze on the beauty of the falls and the bluffs. Near the city are the Falls of Minnehaha, famous in legend and song. Lake Minnetonka is the summer resort of the people, a garden of islands in a crystal sea.

Minneapolis is remarkable as a health resort. Some of its most enterprising citizens first went there on account of weak lungs or pulmonary disease, victims of over mental work and too great business activity. Some of these restored invalids were brought there on their beds. The dry, bracing air arrested the disease, their old appetite came back again, the cough became less distressing, hemorrhages ceased; finally they gained in flesh and strength; and the happiness of their restoration, the beauty of the place, the memories of rekindled hope, and the kindness of friends, induced them to make the city their

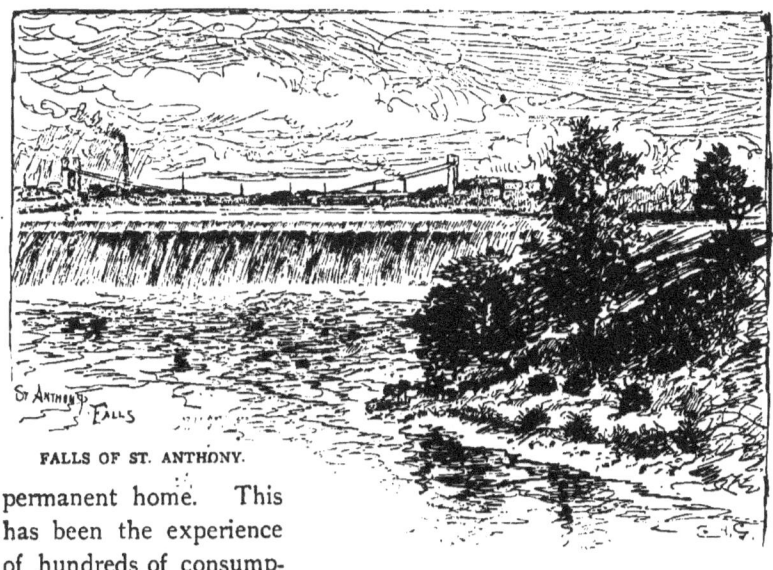

FALLS OF ST. ANTHONY.

permanent home. This has been the experience of hundreds of consumptives who went there in the earlier stages of the disease and of some who came in a condition pronounced hopeless. But all do not recover.

THE STRANGE STORY OF ANTOINE AUGUEL.

In the summer of 1680 Father Hennepin landed on the banks of the Mississippi, near the bluffs where Minneapolis now stands, and rested there to admire the beauty of the waterfall.

"This is one of the loveliest spots I have seen in all my travels," he said. "St. Anthony of Padua has heard my prayers; I will call the cataract the Falls of St. Anthony."

SHORT LINE BRIDGE.

The cool waters fell fifty feet on the hot midsummer day. The soft, friable sandstone, with its light stratum of limestone, over which the river poured, has

FALLS OF MINNEHAHA.

crumbled away since then; and we see now only a series of beautiful cascades where the waters once dashed and foamed, and amber mists rose in the summer sunlight.

The falls were then supposed to be a deity's palace. The god of the Sioux lived there. He sometimes appeared to the Indians in a material form, usually that of a buffalo.

Father Hennepin was accompanied by two adventurers. One of these was a very mysterious man, who bore the name of Picard du Gay, but who was supposed to be Antoine Auguel, from the province of Picardy. He was also called "the Picard."

The Picard had connected himself with Father Hennepin's fortunes in a strange and romantic way. He disappeared at one time mysteriously, it being reported that he had joined the Sioux.

After resting awhile, the resolute explorers took up their canoe and carried it past the falls. As they were doing so their attention was called to five Indians who had come to make offerings to their god. One of these Indians climbed into an oak-tree near the principal fall, and hung there a robe of beaver skin, leaving it for Oanktayhee, as the deity was called.

After placing their canoe in position near the smooth flowing river, Father Hennepin and one of his companions sought rest and food in an Indian lodge, but Antoine Auguel joined the Indians who had come there to sacrifice to the god.

They told him of Lake Minnetonka.

"On the shore of the lake," said one, "there are mounds that were built by a very ancient people who inhabited the country before the Indians; and," he added, "a hermit lives among them, a very young man, who does not grow old, and who came there from the unknown lands."

The Picard asked the Indians to conduct him to the hermit's abode. They consented to do so, and Antoine left Father Hennepin, promising to return on the following day.

When he returned the next day at sunset, he was rebuked by Father Hennepin for having remained so long, and asked what discoveries he had made.

"Father Hennepin," he said, "I have met the most mysterious person of whom I have any knowledge. That person possesses a secret more valuable than gold. I would rather own it than to have the splendors of Versailles. I may tell you of my strange adventure some day, but not now."

The Picard was an altered man from that day. He talked strangely, and at night he dreamed strange dreams. His ambition for adventure forsook him.

At times he would appear to be forgetful of all things around him. Then his downcast eyes would fill with a strange light.

"Fountains! fountains!" he would exclaim. "We must have fountains or die. Die? It maddens me. It makes my brain burn. Oh, could I cool it in that fountain!"

HANGING THE ROBE.

One day he said, —

"Father Hennepin, even you must die."

"Yes," said the priest sadly. "Suppose you were to discover a land of mountains whose bases were gold. What would it profit you if you are to die?"

"The soul will not die," said the priest. "We are souls clothed in the flesh. We shall one day lay the worn-out garment by. There is a better world than this."

"Then to what purpose is all this peril and adventure?"

"For the Church."

"Father Hennepin, I never wish to leave the region of the Sioux. I have made a discovery here. Fountains! fountains! — what was I saying? —*fountains!*"

Strange indeed was the life that these explorers lived on their way to the Wisconsin. The Mississippi flowed calmly on its way, amid wildernesses of green grass and bright flowers, woods full of game, bluffs that in the moonlight appeared like the domes and pinnacles of ruined cathedrals and towers. The rocks were lined with honeysuckles, and the tender leaves of the wild grape-vine formed lovely arbors here and there along the banks.

On their way they met another party of Indians, who told them that they had recently seen five spirits, meaning white men. These proved to be Daniel du Lhut, with four Frenchmen.

The Picard confided to Du Lhut or Duluth the secret he had learned on the shores of Lake Minnetonka. Du Lhut was an ambitious man, full of schemes for wealth. He had built a trading-fort on Lake Superior. He laughed at the Picard's story.

"Antoine Auguel," he said, "you are dreaming; your mind is touched; this is indeed a region of mysteries, but there is no power in all the Americas so mysterious as *that.*"

Duluth was not in the favor of the Canadian government. He was the supposed leader of the *coureurs*

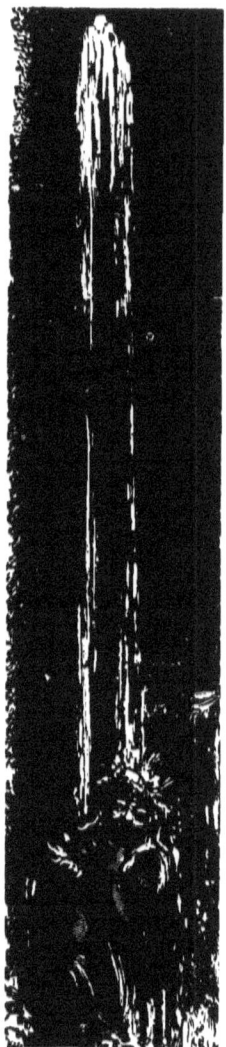

FABLE LAND.

de bois, or independent hunters, who left the settlements and often remained in the forests for years seeking the most valuable furs, with which they supplied the traders without the government sanction. He belonged to the lesser nobles of France, but preferred the wild life of New France to the gayeties and elegances of European civilization.

The mysterious story that Antoine Auguel had told to Duluth haunted the

THE PICARD'S DREAM.

mind of this forest adventurer. One evening, at a meeting of young *coureurs de bois* on the shores of Lake Superior, he chanced to say, —

"The wonders of this country seem to be without limit, and the stories that the Indians tell us are stranger than anything ever heard by the caliphs of Bagdad. But Antoine Auguel, the Picard, once confided to me a story that is more remarkable than anything of which I ever heard or read."

The young hunters demanded the story.

A REMARKABLE DISCOVERY.

Antoine was one day stopping near the Falls of St. Anthony, when he met some Indians who had come to sacrifice to the god of the place. They told him of a lake some miles distant, where they said lived a young hermit who did not grow old. He asked them to conduct him to the hermit's lodge.

They led him to a beautiful lake full of peninsulas and islands. On the shores there were mounds, and among these mounds Antoine was surprised to find a young and exceedingly handsome Spanish cavalier.

LAND FULL OF RUINS.

Antoine demanded of him,—

"Who are you that thus trespass on the dominions of his majesty, the King of France?"

"The world is wide," answered the cavalier, in French. "If I could have my wish I would not trespass upon any earthly dominion, but would gladly leave

this burden of flesh and be with my wife and children, whose spirits live in more blessed spheres than this."

"You seem to be a very young man."

"I am hundreds of years old."

"How can that be?"

"I accompanied Jean Ponce de Leon to Porto Rico. I was then thirty years old. When De Leon resigned the office of Governor of Porto Rico he had begun to grow old.

THE SPANISH CAVALIER.

"There came to him some Indian sages who told him of the Fountain of Youth.

"De Leon never discovered that fountain. *I did.*"

"When and where?"

"Listen.

"After I heard the story of the sages, I continually longed to plunge into the waters of that gifted fountain, and thus be enabled to live forever amid the noble and beautiful scenes of these newly discovered lands.

"I left De Leon on April 3, 1512. About a week before, he had discovered a new land that was wholly covered with flowers. He took possession of it in the name of the Castilian sovereigns, and called it Florida. It seemed to me that such a paradise must contain the fountain of which the Indians had told, and I resolved never again to go on board of the ships. I deserted as soon as I could separate myself from the commander. I did not find the fountain in that flowery land.

"Then I began to wander. I passed along the coast, first towards the north, then towards the west, then towards the south. I came at last to a land full of

LAKE MINNETONKA.

ruins; it was beautiful beyond description; it seemed to have been a home of the gods.

"Fountains were there, water-gods, naiads, and beautiful temples, under the tropic trees. I bathed in them. I bathed in every fountain I met, and I dipped myself in the Fountain of Youth."

"Where?"

"I cannot tell; nor can I tell which of the hundred fountains in which I bathed was the magical fountain. One of them was, for I have never grown old.

"Thirty years passed, when I saw on the coast a Spanish vessel. I hailed her and was taken on board. I returned to Andalusia, to the Gaudalquivir.

"My wife was old and withered. My children were seemingly older than myself; they were gray. I told them my story; they treated me with derision, and forced me away from my own home.

COUREUR DE BOIS

"Then one by one they died. I saw the grave open again and again until all my family were gone. I longed to go, too. But I did not grow old.

"I returned to America. I wished to flee from my land, from society, from the face of man. I again deserted, and ascended a great and unknown river. I left my canoe at yonder falls. It went into decay a hundred years ago. I found this beautiful lake and these green mounds in summer time. I was sure society would never find me here, and here I built my lodge and live.

"The beautiful summers and the cold winters come and go, but I see only the faces of the red men. I am never hungry; I am never cold. I have but one wish; it haunts me continually: I would that I could die."

The young *coureurs de bois* listened to the tale with intense interest, and some of them plied every possible inquiry in regard to what the hermit had said of the country where the magical fountain had been found.

Four of these young men went into the forest and were never heard of again.

From time to time the visitors to Lake Minnetonka have seen a strange figure in a boat on the lake. The oars of the boat fly from them like wings. Should you see a flying boatman on the lake, if you do not believe him to be the Spanish cavalier, you may still allow this story to recall to your mind the old historic associations of beautiful Minneapolis.

CHAPTER X.

DAKOTA.

DAKOTA. — JAMES RIVER VALLEY. — NEW TOWNS. — STORIES.

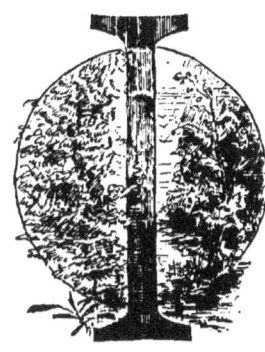
T was a long ride from Minneapolis to Aberdeen, Dakota, but through a region of wonderful fertility, filled with crystal lakes and young towns. The hill country near the Sioux Reservation was very beautiful, and everywhere the air was like a sparkling cordial; and fancy kindled and glowed at the thought that here the great empire of the Northwest was just beginning to rise; that in the emigrant wagons were pioneers of cities, and the canvas of each prairie schooner was the sails of a new Mayflower.

The James River Valley is one of those fertile regions which are sure to become a centre of agricultural wealth, enterprise, and intelligence. Valley? It stretches from Huron to Ordway, a distance of nearly one hundred miles. It is from forty to sixty miles wide. It is as large as some of the most populous Eastern States. The James River flows through its centre; it is walled by picturesque mountains; the famous White Stone Hill Battle-Field is here, near the young town of Frederic, which is leaping into life. It embraces the counties of Brown, Spink, and Beadle, and the unpronounceable lake of Tchanchicuha, in Brown County.

The cars were full of land agents and immigrants. The former,

FOUNTAIN OF YOUTH.

as is always the case, were very enthusiastic over the prospects of the newly opened region of the Northwest.

"A wonderful valley this," said one of these men to Tommy Toby. "A man might mount his plough and turn a furrow eighty miles long."

"A man might mount his plough and ride to the Pacific," thought Tommy, but he did not say so to the enterprising agent.

"Is the land fertile?" he asked.

"Fertile!" said the agent, leaping from his seat as though he had taken a shock from a battery. "Look yonder and yonder; when Nature made that land she exhausted all her powers, as the poet says."

If the poet said so, the matter would seem to be settled beyond dispute in the mind of this susceptible land dealer. There was no question that the country was inviting, whatever any one might say.

"What does it usually cost to make a farm on government land?" asked Herman of the agent, who, if he was over-enthusiastic, was really intelligent.

"It costs fourteen dollars to enter one hundred and sixty acres of land."

"How much to bring a part of it, say fifty acres, under cultivation the first year," continued Herman.

"About two dollars and fifty cents per acre," answered the agent.

"For example, you have one hundred acres ploughed in early June. You could sow it with flax, and it would probably yield ten bushels to the acre, which would bring you one dollar per bushel, or one thousand dollars."

"What would be the profit?"

"Your account would stand something like this," said the agent, writing with a pencil on a card: —

Cost of land	$14.00
Agent's fees	10.00
Breaking land	250.00
Seed	60.00
Cultivating	70.00
Harvesting	200.00
	$604.00
Value of crop	$1,000.00

"Your profits ought to amount to over three hundred dollars, after the cost of marketing is deducted; it might be more than that, for some land yields from fifteen to eighteen bushels per acre."

"Is this land being rapidly taken?"

"Yes, and strangely enough the Western people are emigrating to the West. A large number of the new settlers are from Iowa, Illinois, and Michigan. Nearly all enter three hundred and twenty acres, and many of them buy as much more land of the railroads. The immigrants from abroad are intelligent, thrifty people. They have purpose and character. Adventurers, gamblers, and men without a purpose do not go to an agricultural country to earn a living by honest exertion."

"Is there much land that remains for new settlers."

"Much!" the man started up again. "Why, in Brown County alone there are one million acres."

"In one county?"

"Yes, Dakota is nearly twice the size of England and about as large as France. It would swallow up New England."

"Aberdeen!" called the conductor.

"The Western people all seem to understand how to make England, France, and New England appear cheap and small," said Tommy to Gentleman Jo.

"New Englanders find here that what they lack is territory."

"And here it is," said the agent, with a smile, as the cars stopped.

Aberdeen is a railroad town which has started into life in the heart of the James River Valley. It is in Brown County, which was organized in 1880. Only about two years ago this county, with its skeleton towns, was occupied by a band of Sioux Indians, under a chief who bore the picturesque name of Drifting Goose. In 1881 two lines of railway entered this county, the Chicago, Milwaukee, and St. Paul, and the Chicago and Northwestern. Another line came threading its way over the Coteau Hills; cabins and sod houses followed all the lines, and where these lines cross sprung up Aberdeen. Only about two years old, it has a fine hotel, two newspapers, and is erecting churches and schoolhouses. The public school building is to cost five thousand dollars.

On leaving the train, the Class were surprised to see a young man waving his hat towards them from a rustic vehicle drawn by two fine horses. He had a brown face under a broad-brimmed hat, wore a blouse and baggy trousers, and seemed in the highest possible spirits.

The Class stopped.

The young man waved his hat again.

"Long live America!"

"Intoxicated," said Tommy.

"They said that there were no fast young men in this country."

"Three cheers for Massachusetts and the good old Academy of Yule!" shouted the young man.

"George Howe!" exclaimed Tommy.

The fat horses came trotting up to the station. An expression of surprise filled the boys' faces.

"George!"
"George!"
"George!"

"We thought you were drunk," said Tommy, "and here we are come to bring you a Sunday-school library."

"I have ridden all the way from Frederic to meet you, and you give me a bad name before I can grasp your hand," said George.

There were warm graspings of hands, and the manly young man shed tears as the meeting brought back the memories and revived the affections of the old Newton school.

"THREE CHEERS FOR MASSACHUSETTS!"

The Class went to the hotel. After a good meal George took the boys on a long excursion up the valley.

How strange it was! What an immense expanse of level land covered with flowers and walled with far hills! It looked like a wide lake of sunshine. The hills seemed some twenty miles away.

"Those are the Missouri Coteaus," said George, at one point of the journey, pointing to the Northwest.

"Can we ride to them this afternoon?" asked Tommy.

"How far away do you think they are?"

"Ten or twenty miles."

"More than fifty," said George. "The clear air of the prairie deceives the eye of a person from the East."

The party returned to the town on the following day.

"This is hardly like Æneas discovering Dido building Carthage," said George; "but history will make a long mark here, as odd and crude as all things may look to you."

EARLY SETTLERS IN DAKOTA.

"Not much like Æneas and Dido indeed," said Tommy, as two engines gave terrific shrieks, and the horses started off with a velocity that required all the strength of the driver to curb.

The Class went up the valley to Frederic, a town scarcely a year old and not found on the map. It is situated on the bank of the Maple River, which is famous for the purity and softness of its water. The town was building on a slightly inclined plain sloping towards the west and south. Nowhere but in the West could such a miracle of transformation be seen. Last year hardly a settlement; this year not found on the map; car loads of immigrants arriving, the public houses full of enthusiastic people, the lumber supply unequal to the demand, nearly a hundred people locating claims in a single week; next year what?—a town, and the next perhaps a city.

George had already made himself well known in the new towns in the valley. In one of them he had organized a reading club, and in another a Sunday-school.

The Class visited George's Sunday-school. It was held in a plain room of a new house, but the children had happy, intelligent faces, and seemed eager for instruction. George was already beginning to multiply good influences, and Master Lewis was pleased to mark this result of right intention and good character.

George had written several times to Master Lewis about his school, and the teacher had sent him Bibles, music books, and instructive papers for the work. The Class, at Master Lewis's suggestion, had collected quite a number of books to give to George to begin a Sunday-school and village library. The boys had brought these books with them.

Master Lewis had bought for the school Smith's Bible Dictionary, and Kitto's Cyclopedia of Biblical Knowledge. He was asked by George to address the scholars.

He took Kitto's noble work and held it up before the school in silence as the text of an object lesson. He then related a story.

MASTER LEWIS'S STORY.

You see this large volume. I hope you will read it. It is one of the best sources of information about the Bible in the language.

Give me your attention, and I will tell you something about the writer of this book. The story may have a lesson for you.

We will visit his home. The place, Plymouth, England, with its smoky streets and foamy harbor. The time, the first part of the present century. The house, a hovel; the family tattered, distressed, with hungry faces, hopeless, woe-begone.

The boy John Kitto. He is tender at heart, but he has no friends; he is a lover of books, but he finds no regular teacher.

He makes the best use of the few books that he has; he reads them, and spells them and learns them with the quenchless zeal of one whose life is so sunless, so dreary. He spends his days in carrying brick and mortar to his father, who is a working mason. He is slender for such hard work, and young, — only ten or twelve. There are no daisied walks for his bare feet, no fields sprinkled with flowers and gladdened with birds. He

PLYMOUTH.

sees little but the windy harbor, and hears little save the complaints of the wretched at home, and far off the moaning of the waves on the bar.

Poor little boy! He is thirteen now, and he works at carrying slate up the ladder to the roof, not an easy nor a quiet employment for a poor little boy. One day he becomes weary. In stepping from the ladder to the roof his foot slips, he loses his balance, he falls. Thirty feet fell that poor little boy with his burden of slate.

He struck on a paved court. They took him up and carried him home. They thought him dying and said he would die. We should not wonder if they hoped he would die, for the family could hardly find bread for those who toiled from sun to sun ; much more for a helpless invalid.

Would you like to hear his own story of this accident?

"Of what followed," he said, " I know nothing. For one moment indeed I awoke from a death-like state, and found that my father, attended by a crowd of people, was bearing me homeward in his arms, but I had no recollection of what had happened, and at once relapsed into a state of unconsciousness.

"In this state I remained for a fortnight. Those days were a blank in my life ; when I awoke one morning to consciousness, it was as from a night of sleep.

" My hearing was entirely gone. I saw the people around me talking to one another, but thought that, out of regard to my feeble condition, they spoke in whispers, because I heard them not. I asked for a book I had been reading on the day of my fall. I was answered by signs.

"' Why do you not speak ?' I asked. 'Pray let me have the book.'

" A member of the family wrote upon a slate that the book had been taken away by its owner.

" ' But why do you write ?' I asked. 'Why do you not speak ? '

" Those around me exchanged looks of concern. Then the slate was handed me with the awful words, ' YOU ARE DEAF.'"

Poor, deaf, and little cared for !

He could not help his father now. But he resolved to work, even on the bed of pain. He borrowed books and began to store his mind. This he continued to do until his strength in a measure returned again. His hearing never returned. The world was all silent to him like a dumb show.

But he lived; why, no one could tell. We think not because he was wanted in the world, for he was a burden. His parents were unable to support him any longer, and they made known their situation to the overseers of the poor, who took the deaf little lad away from his home and what little charms it had, — it must have had some, — and put him in the poor-house or work-house. Here he was taught to make shoes. He worked hard, and he trusted in God, and — he knew not why — he spent every leisure moment in improving his mind. He was next apprenticed to a shoemaker, a bad man, who had no feeling for the sad-hearted deaf boy, and who used him like a dog. He treated him so ill that the magistrates interfered, and took him away. The lad used to work sixteen hours a day, but in the remaining eight he still took an hour for the improvement of his mind.

At last he began to write for a Plymouth journal, and his ability so excited public attention that people began to feel kindly towards him, and to assist him. They lent him Greek books, and he learned Greek ; books on modern tongues and the sciences, and he mastered them. He became a teacher, a traveller, a theologian, an Oriental scholar, and the author of books to be found in every library.

Reviewing the past, he says : "It does somewhat move me to look back upon that poor deaf boy, in his utter loneliness, devoting himself to objects in which none around him could sympathize, and to pursuits which none could understand. When I was a shoemaker's apprentice, I worked sixteen hours out of the twenty-four, and my heart gave way. Now that I look back upon this time, the amount of study which I did contrive to get through, under these circumstances, amazes and confounds me."

The world is full of disappointed men. The poor deaf boy of Plymouth work-house is not among them. He sowed in the darkness ; he is reaping in the light. I think that no scholar in this school will ever have so hard a lot as this. If any should, remember the lesson of this boy's life.

"Commit thy way unto the Lord ! trust also in Him, and he will bring it to pass."

The Class were taken by stage from Frederic to Jamestown, thence by the Great Northern Pacific Railroad to Bismarck, and thence to Montana.

The Northern Pacific Railroad will soon become the most wonderful avenue of travel on the continent. When completed it will extend from Duluth, at the western end of Lake Superior, to Puget Sound, in Washington Territory, a distance of about seventeen hundred miles. It will be a principal line of communication with the valley of the Red River of the North, the James River Valley, the grain region of Dakota, the cattle kingdom of Montana, and the pleasure resorts of the Yellowstone National Park. It will contribute to the growth of some new Chicago and Minneapolis which must soon rise in the great chain of cities, perhaps on the Missouri River. Will the new city be Bismarck?

A TRESTLE ON THE NORTHERN PACIFIC.

Jamestown is beautifully situated on an almost level plateau. It is surrounded by hills, and the river flows through its centre. It is growing with wonderful rapidity.

Bismarck is built on a slope of land about a mile from the Missouri River. It has excellent churches and schools. It must soon become a flourishing city, perhaps the next great city of the Northwest.

JERRY SLACK AGAIN.

The emigrants in all of these new towns were full of confidence and enthusiasm. They seemed to live in the future. They beheld hope's rainbows everywhere. Their pride was an honest one, and their purpose to lay a good foundation for future prosperity a most worthy one.

"What do you find for amusements?" asked Tommy of a young man in Ordway.

"I am so taken up with my work and interested in the growth of these parts that I have n't thought anything about amusements since I came West," he said. "I used to go to amusements when I was in Portland, Maine, and spent a good deal of time and money on them. But my thoughts here all run to securing a good home for my family. I do not think I should have amounted to much in the East. To tell the truth, I never knew what it was to *live* until I married and came West. I am happy and do not have to *hire* amusements."

"Jerry Slack and his Money-Pot," said Tommy to Gentleman Jo, as the young man turned away to go to his home.

Home? It was a house of plain boards, of only two rooms, and costing less than one hundred dollars. Yet he was "happy," and did not have to "*hire* amusements."

"A young man should find his amusement in his purpose in life and his business," said Gentleman Jo.

AUNT ABBY.

The Class met with one person, and only one, we believe, who did not enter into the enthusiasm of Western enterprise. It was "Aunt Abby," at Jamestown. She had encountered the one terror of a Dakota winter, a blizzard.

"A wonderful country," said Gentleman Jo to her.

"I should think so," said she. "Did you ever see it *blow?*"

"No; not since I was a mail agent. The weather seems delightful."

"You ought to have been here last March. I have a son in a place called Milbank. He wrote to me that they did not have the catarrh and bronchitis in Dakota, and that the winter in the Jim River Valley, as he called it, was just like Indian summer, or had been up to February.

"Now I live at Providence, Rhode Island, and have the bronchitis *awful*, especially in the winter. It was very bad last fall and during the early part of winter, so I thought I would just pack up and go to Milbank, the place of Indian summer and no catarrh.

"James — he's my boy — never got along very well in Rhode Island, but he wrote me that he'd secured a 'quarter of a section' of land, whatever that might mean, and had built a house. *That* sounded enterprising. Well, I started and I got there, though the last part of the journey was rather distressing for a woman of my age.

"Well, the climate was beautiful, and my bronchitis disappeared. James's house would n't have made much of a show on College Hill, in Providence, but he seemed contented. I began to join in the every-day chorus of the praises of the new country, when one March day it began to *blow*. And it blew and blew. Then there came a snow-storm, and it blew so hard that it blew the snow all to pieces, and they called it a blizzard.

"James had n't a very full supply of fuel, so we had to go to bed to keep warm. And James's wife, after we all got into our beds, said she would entertain us by telling stories.

"Her stories were about people who got all snowed up and were dug out by bears and catamounts and wolves. They were worse than the old-fashioned witch stories. The next day we found ourselves all snowed up, and had to lie abed most of the time for warmth. I expected we would be dug out by wolves or some kind of wild creatures, though James said that there was nothing of the kind around.

"The next night we heard a *howl*. It upset my nerves entirely. I resolved if ever I saw daylight and a clear path to the cars, to *go*. It was a dog that howled, but *what's the difference as long as you did n't know?* In a few days I got on to a freight train, and went to a town where there was a good hotel. Then I came here. I would n't stay here for nothin' only my bronchitis does n't trouble me."

In contrast with Aunt Abby's experience, Wyllys Wynn met an

A BLIZZARD.

old English lady near Bismarck, whose homely but touching story gave him a subject for a poem.

OLD WORLD FRIENDS IN THE NEW.

"I was very poor in England," she said, "and I was left a widow early in life. My sons had but a hard prospect in the old country, and they and their families came to New York.

"At last they sent for their old mother. How it made my heart rejoice! I parted from my daughter and friends at Queenstown, but I was happy because I expected to meet the Old World friends in the New.

"We came West. *Their* prospects are good, and I am contented. I shall go to another world soon. I am ready. I hope I may meet there the Old World friends. I often think of the evening I sailed from Queenstown, and somehow it reminds me of a better world than this."

QUEENSTOWN BAY.

I sailed away from Queenstown Bay
  In the evening calm and clear,
But my thoughts went back o'er the dim sea track,
  To the lights round Queenstown Pier.
We said, that day, in Queenstown Bay,
  Ere Ireland sunk from view,
We shall meet again, beyond the main,
  The Old World friends in the New.
    Far, far away
    From Queenstown Bay,
    From Queenstown Bay.

The wind blew free o'er the refluent sea,
  The warm land breeze of June,
And far a-west, o'er the water's breast,
  Hung the silver bow of the moon.
Then friends, divorced by the fading coast,
  Came back in memories true,
But the thought was sweet that we soon should meet
  The Old World friends in the New.
    Far, far away
    From Queenstown Bay,
    From Queenstown Bay.

The lights again, o'er the ocean plain,
  Slowly began to rise,
And the land breeze fair stole through the air
  Like the balms of Paradise.
And thick the lights on the home-crowned heights
  Round Castle Garden grew ;
And waited for me o'er the havened sea,
  The Old World friends in the New.
      Far, far away
      From Queenstown Bay,
      From Queenstown Bay.

I shall sail once more for an unseen shore ;
  I shall part with friends most dear,
As we parted that night in the fading light
  That glimmered round Queenstown Pier.
And again will arise, under cloudless skies,
  A havened city in view ;
Do there wait for me, beyond the sea,
  Some Old World friends in the New,
      As on that day
      When I sailed away
      From Queenstown Bay ?

CHAPTER XI.

WONDER-LAND.

THE YELLOWSTONE NATIONAL PARK. — A MARVELLOUS REGION. — HOODOO LAND.

"WE are now on our way to a region to which lovers of nature will one day journey from all parts of the world," said Gentleman Jo, as the Class mounted the stage-coach for Fort Ellis.

From Fort Ellis the Class took saddle-horses for the wonder-land of which the boys had for six months read and dreamed.

It was a perfect day in July as the boys rode along the left bank of the Yellowstone. The air was dry and bracing, the earth was a sea of flowers in which the horses seemed to wade, and a light, golden atmosphere hung over all, — a clear, unnatural brightness such as a poet-artist sometimes imparts to the canvas. On the second day of the journey they passed the Devil's Slide, which consists of parallel walls of stone extending from the summit of a mountain to the valley below. On the evening of the same day they reached the first natural wonder of the Park, the mammoth Hot Springs of Gardiner River.

Their approach to the springs opened to them a scene never to be forgotten. Across a high plateau appeared a snow-white mountain. Over it hung a mist like a purple veil, with fringes that gathered their colors from the sunset

The boys stopped their horses, and waited for Gentleman Jo, who was riding in the rear of the party, leaving the leadership to a guide from Fort Ellis.

"What mountain is that?" they asked, pointing to the white elevation with its truly royal canopy.

"A mountain of hot springs," said Gentleman Jo.

"It looks like a mountain of a fable," said Wyllys.

"Its history is like a fable," said Gentleman Jo. "The springs made the mountain."

"How?"

"The springs have poured through the crust of the earth for ages, and constantly deposited a mineral substance in the form of rising mounds. The mounds made hills, and the hills made a mountain. The summit of the mountain is still an area of boiling springs, and is still slowly rising. The bright mist that hangs over it is a vapor from the springs.

"This story differs from the fables in books. You can still see the springs building the mountain."

As the Class approached more closely to the mountain, it seemed to be changed into gems.

"A transformation in Fable Land," said Gentleman Jo. "The springs are heated by subterranean fires; the water is boiled in natural furnaces. The hot water pours over the ridge of the mountain and is caught in reservoirs or pools. These pools overflow, and the water is again caught in pools on lower terraces of the mountain, which also overflow, and pour the water down to still lower terraces."

"And the gems that we see —"
"Are reservoirs of boiling water. Each reservoir or pool has a

porcelain rim, and emits a vapor in intensity according to the heat of the water. The sun transforms the whole into a scene of beauty,

like St. Peter's illuminated. The top of the mountain, as you can see, is like an imaginary palace or a temple of a sun god."

The next day the boys saw the springs from another point of view. The level rays of the sun lighted up each pool, and the mountain, glimmering with every color and variation of color, seemed like a stupendous temple of gems. Night brought to the scene a wonderful transformation. The half moon made every pool a fountain of pearls and diamonds.

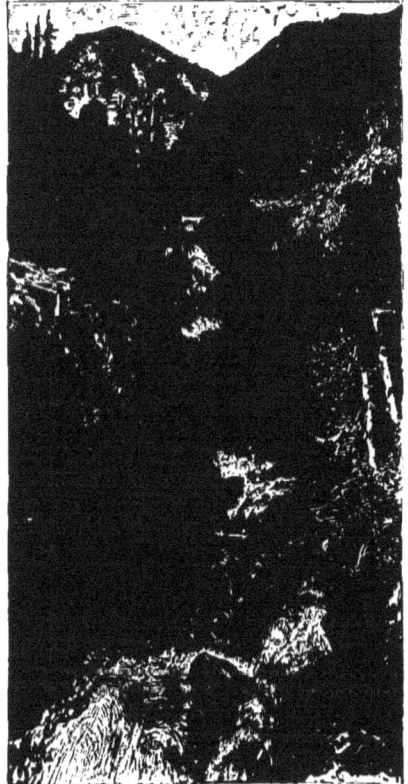
MARY'S VEIL CASCADE.

"One might go up to the Celestial City from here," said Wyllys. "Do you believe that Jacob in the desert ever saw a ladder like that?"

A cloud came over the moon and the vision faded. "As all earthly enchantments are likely to disappear," remarked Gentleman Jo.

The Class spent the hours of rest in a tent which the guides pitched each afternoon in some sheltered situation. Gentleman Jo arranged everything admirably for the comfort of the travellers; and health, cheerful spirits, and good fortune attended them wherever they went.

One night, as the boys were resting in their tent near Tower Fall, while on a detour to the region of Mt. Washburn, they heard a fierce, wild scream. It was electrical.

THE GROTTO AND FAN GEYSER.

"What is that?" asked Tommy.
"A mountain lion," said one of the guides.
"What does he want?" asked Tommy.
"A boy," said the guide.
"How would I do?'
"Suppose you go out and see."
Another ear-piercing cry broke the stillness of the night.
"I would not like to be in this tent alone," said Tommy. "Of all howls I ever heard, that is the most terrible. If an animal were to chase me and send after me one howl like that, I should drop as though I were shot. I hope the tent is well guarded."

Tower Fall issues from a pine-shaded mountain gorge, and is partly surrounded by many colored sandstone towers, some of which rise two hundred

TOWER FALL.

or more feet above the foaming waters. The cascade and its surroundings seem like the ruin of a vast fortress or temple.

Passing Mt. Washburn, which rises eleven thousand feet above the sea level, and which is nearly twice as high as Mt. Washington and almost as high as Mont Blanc, the Class encamped one night in the Grand Cañon of the Yellowstone.

The most wonderful waterfall scenery of the continent is here. Following the Yellowstone River amid the marvellous surprises of the mountain walls, the Class began to regard the cascades with growing interest, especially as each one presented wilder, bolder, and more fantastic features than the one preceding. The guides at last pointed to a fall leaping one hundred and forty feet into a cavern.

YELLOWSTONE RIVER.

The boys wished to rest here and enjoy the beauty of the remarkable scene.

"That is nothing," said the guides. "Come on."

The boys hurried after the guides, wondering what more remarkable exhibition of nature could be awaiting them. In about fifteen minutes the guides shouted. The boys followed them closely and expectantly.

Suddenly there burst upon the view of the party a stupendous scene. It was a waterfall three times as high as Niagara, and having such a velocity that the waters were turned into foam on the way to the awful channel in the mountain walls. The boys started back from the view of the pine-clad precipices, rocky peaks, and pinnacles that make the framework for this terrific feat of the Yellowstone.

"It is like a view of eternity," said Wyllys.

"It exhibits the possibilities of nature," said Gentleman Jo.

"It shows the possibilities of the soul," said Master Lewis. "It is like an allegory. It gives me a sense of time and space not before realized."

"I feel as though I had been too greatly overpowered," said Wyllys. "The sense of it is too much for my mind; I have felt so before, when I have looked through the telescope; I wish to glance at it and turn away."

The falls of the Grand Cañon of the Yellowstone descend through numerous cascades and the two gigantic cataracts, a distance of nearly one thousand feet. The walls of the cañon are brilliantly colored, and the halls of the Alhambra are but miniature splendors in comparison with these water-worn caverns, which seem like throne-rooms of the gods of fable.

Says P. W. Norris, superintendent of the Park, of these palace pictures, frescos, and carvings of Nature:—

PHILIP CASCADE.

The Twin Falls trail reaches the river amidst rocky walls whose cornice-like formation possesses a variety and brilliancy of tint and coloring, matchless and enchanting, which it is impossible to describe, and which to be understood and appreciated must be seen. Indeed, in many portions of the cañons the coloring of the walls is the principal charm. The Grand Cañon of the Colorado is longer and deeper than this; the Yosemite more accessible, and to some, perhaps, more attractive, while other cañons are more ragged, weird, and yawning; but no known cañon so combines magnitude, meanderings, foamy, emerald waters, hissing hot springs, spouting geysers, and inimitably beautiful tinting of its walls as the peerless Cañon of the Yellowstone.

From the Grand Cañon, the Class passed through a region as dismal as was ever pictured to the mind of Dante when composing

YELLOWSTONE LAKE.

the "Inferno." The earth bubbled with hot springs; the air had the odors of sulphur, and at last a sulphur mountain rose directly from a sulphurous plain, having two boiling caldrons at its foot. The air became stifling.

But the sulphurous mountain was not the end of this region of horrors. A few miles beyond it were volcanoes spouting mud. The vapors from these were black and formed an appalling cloud. The ground was at intervals shaken by dreadful explosions.

About eight miles from this Inferno, the Class reached the moun-

MUD VOLCANOES.

tain sea called Yellowstone Lake. Thence the guides travelled westward some thirty miles, leading the party to the famous Geyser Basin of Fire-hole River.

A MARVELLOUS SPECTACLE.

"Geyser land!" shouted a guide.

It was early morning. The Class emerged from a green forest into view of a snowy plain. The boys had mounted the saddle by daylight, and had followed the guides in eager expectation of every moment seeing the gigantic fountains of which they had read and heard.

It was a bright morning. As soon as the guide shouted, the boys hurried forward their horses, and each one uttered a loud exclamation as the region of fountains met his view. A world of geysers lay before them, each fountain tossing its glittering water high in the air and melting into spray and many colored vapors.

The basin was a thousand acres in extent, and white and glimmering.

"The fountains of all the palace gardens of Europe would not equal a scene like that," said Wyllys. "This *is* a National Park, and one worthy of the country."

The Class proceeded to the Great Geyser Basin, where a more marvellous spectacle was to be seen. In this basin are fourteen immense geysers and some forty prismatic hot springs, beside countless steam jets.

YELLOWSTONE LAKE.

The geysers are intermittent in their action. The columns of water forced into the air vary from fifty to nearly three hundred feet. The longer the geysers rest, the more grand and lofty are the columns when the action begins.

The Class entered the Great or Upper Basin in the afternoon. The boys had hardly left their horses when a guide called to them, "The Cathedral is playing."

The earth trembled.

A cathedral of water rose in the sun, and vanished.

A roaring caused the boys to check their exclamations of wonder.

"Now for Old Faithful," said the guide. "It spouts every ten minutes. See the steam beginning to rise."

Old Faithful seemed like a giant in the throes of agony. Presently a column of water rose some fifteen feet.

"OLD FAITHFUL."

The boys were disappointed.
"Wait," said the guide.

GEYSER LAND.

The earth shook as though some tremendous power beneath it were seeking vent.

Suddenly a column of water rose nearly one hundred feet in height.

The earth shook again; steam came hissing from the crater.

Then an amazing column of water rose to a height of more than two hundred feet and stood like a monument in the sun. All the air grew bright with many colored vapors; geysers were playing on every hand, and presently every eye was directed towards the heavens.

"The air is full of broken rainbows," said Wyllys. "This is wonder-land indeed."

"What is the cause of the geysers?" asked Tommy of Gentleman Jo.

"The snows on the mountains melt and fill the underground rivers. The Yellowstone Park is a region of extinct volcanoes. The furnaces of these volcanoes still burn under the crust of the earth. When the mountain streams reach these volcanic furnaces the water is heated and seeks vent. Hence the geysers."

GOBLIN LAND.

Only a few people except Indians are familiar with the Hoodoo region or Goblin Land. It lies near Hoodoo Mountain, which is more than ten thousand feet high, and has the appearance of a vast graveyard filled with colossal monuments. These stone shafts are called *Hoodoos*.

The late superintendent of the park, Mr. Norris, thus describes this ghostly region, which will soon be opened by a good road to the excursionists who will flock to the place in summer when the Northern Pacific Railroad is completed : —

While probably never itself a crater, Hoodoo Mountain is evidently of volcanic origin, and was eroded into its present form. Upon its southern face it is still changing. Here, extending from five hundred to fifteen hundred feet below the summit, the frosts and storms of untold ages in an Alpine climate have worn

INDIAN AND HIS BRIDE.

about a dozen labyrinths of countless deep, narrow, tortuous channels amid the long, slender, tottering pillars, shafts, and spires of the conglomerate breccia and other remaining volcanic rocks.

In shape these Hoodoos are unlike anything elsewhere known, being a cross between the usual spire and steeple form, and the slender-based and flat, tottering, table-topped sandstone monuments near the Garden of the Gods, in Colorado; and while lacking the symmetry and beauty of these, surpass both in wild, weird fascination.

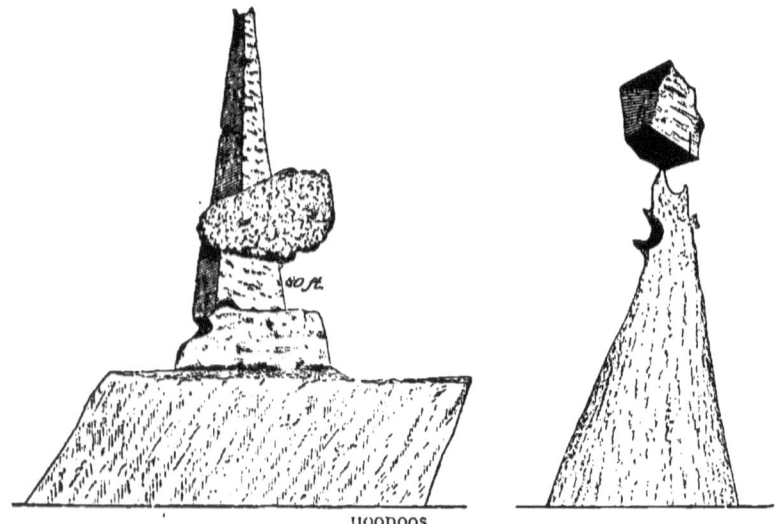

HOODOOS.

Here the sharp-cornered fragments of rocks of nearly every size, form, formation, and shade of coloring, by a peculiar volcanic cement attached sidewise, endwise, and upon the tops, sides, and, apparently, unsupported, upon each other, represent every form, garb, and posture of gigantic human beings, as well as of birds, beasts, and reptiles. In fact, nearly every form, animate or inanimate, real or chimerical, ever actually seen or conjured by the imagination, may here be observed.

Language does not suffice to properly describe these peculiar formations. Sketches may probably do something, and photographs more, to convey a conception of their remarkable character; but actual observation is absolutely necessary to adequately impress the mind with the wild, unearthly appearance of these eroded Hoodoos of the Goblin Land.

These monuments are from fifty to two or three hundred feet in height, with narrow, tortuous passages between them, which sometimes are tunnels through permanent snow or ice fields where the big-horn sheep hide in safety ; while the ceaseless but ever-changing moans of the wild winds seem to chant fitting requiems to these gnome-like monuments of the legendary Indian gods.

Another feature of the Hoodoo region is worthy of more attention than it is here possible to give. I refer to the numerous huge dikes which trend uniformly in parallel lines nearly north and south, unaffected in course, size, or character by yawning cañons or the thousands of feet of craggy mountain sides, to their snowy summits, ever standing high above the softer and deeper disintegrating volcanic formations between them. While all basalt, obsidian, and other columnar formations observed within the Park, when found "in place," are uniformly vertical or radiating, these dikes, although as clearly columnar, are in every observed instance positively horizontal, very hard, and not friable, and part, in columns entire, across the dikes, thus appearing like gigantic steps ascending the cañon and mountain sides.

What a field will the Yellowstone Park open to the artist, poet, and story-writer! What multitudes of people will visit it in the future, people from all lands! How it will form a part of the unknown history of our nation! What historic episodes may be celebrated on this marvellous pleasure ground of the Empire of the West!

The Territories of Wyoming and Idaho have little written history. Dakota will become peopled with wheat-growers, and then emigration from the Atlantic and Pacific will meet on the common ground of this golden empire. The rich soil of Wyoming will be turned into cattle farms, and Idaho's mines into silver farms.

The Territory of Wyoming was formed by an act of Congress in 1868. It has an area as great as the States of New York, Pennsylvania, and New Jersey combined. It is a region of vast plains sheltered by mountain walls. These plains have an average elevation of about six thousand feet above the sea level. Fremont's Peak is twelve thousand feet high, and Cloud Peak fourteen thousand feet high. No Territory has more beautiful or extensive water-courses.

Wyoming has a wonderful climate. It is likely to become a health-resort of invalids from all the States that border on the coast. It is warmed by the currents of air from the West that come through the gateways of the broken mountains. Hence these lofty plains have as soft and lovely an atmosphere as the Pacific isles.

Utah has a semi-tropical climate. Its soil is rich in minerals; it is a part of that great undeveloped empire whose riches it will take a century to comprehend. Strange as it may seem, the much larger part of the settlers of Utah come here from lands beyond the sea. Nine tenths of the people are Mormons, and these represent nearly all European nations, and some of the Pacific islands.

From the Yellowstone Park the Class connected with the railroad for Salt Lake City by a long stage ride. Among the passengers was a very agreeable Northern lady who had been a teacher in Idaho. The Class entertained her with their stories, and at last Tommy Toby ventured to ask her to relate some of her experiences in the new country.

"I have had some rather novel experiences," said the Idaho school-ma'am, "as have several of my friends who have taught schools in the West. I had a friend who taught a school in Wyoming, and among the visitors was — a bear."

"How did she receive him?"

"She heard a noise in the cloak-room or entry, and thought it was one of the scholar's parents. Presently there was a rattling among the scholars' dinner-pails that were left in the room.

"'The 'mittee man,' said one of the scholars.

"But the ''mittee' man did not rap. There was another rattling among the dinner-pails. She slowly opened the door leading from the school-room to the entry, and found the outside door open, and what she supposed to be a man in a fur coat in the entry. A little girl left her seat and pushed her head through the door. She drew it back very quickly, like a shuttle, and said, —

"'It's a *bear!*'

"The teacher, as you may suppose, closed the door very suddenly, and suspended the exercises of the school until the visitor went away, which he did after devouring the con-

"IT'S A BEAR!"

tents of the dinner-pails. The next day bruin called again, but he never went away again, as one of the ' 'mittee ' men was there to receive him."

CHAPTER XII.

THE STORY OF MORMONISM.

TRANSLATING THE BIBLE. — BRIGHAM YOUNG AT THE GREAT SALT LAKE. — THE END OF JOSEPH SMITH. — CAÑON LAND. — A JOURNEY TO SHADOW LAND.

IN the early part of the present century there lived in Cherry Vale, New York, a clergyman by the name of Solomon Spaulding. His health failed, and he sought to lighten his hours of illness by the composition of a romance which he entitled "The Manuscript Found." He was a person of literary and historic tastes, and he entertained the theory that the American Indians were the descendants of the lost ten tribes of Israel. This theory he sought to illustrate in the religious tale, and he attributed the book to an ancient prophet called "Mormon."

The intellect of a person in decline is often brilliant, and Mr. Spaulding's romance developed into a highly imaginative and extended narrative. Much of it was written at New Salem, Ohio, to which Mr. Spaulding removed from New York. There were Indian mounds there that aided his glowing fancy.

"His sole object," said his wife after his decease, "in writing this imaginary history was to amuse himself and his neighbors."

He little knew or dreamed of the evil uses to which this pleasing fiction would be assigned.

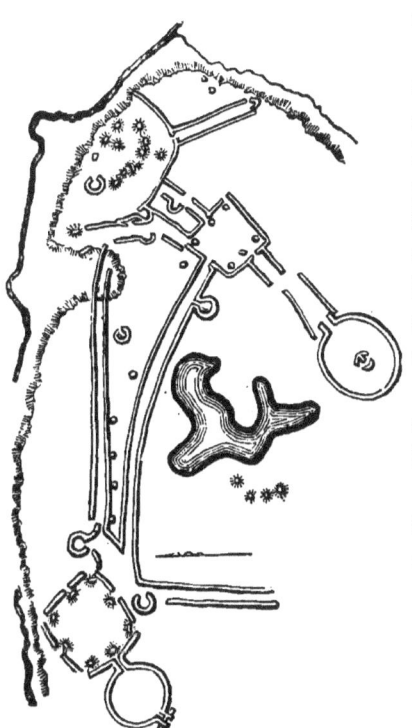

INDIAN MOUNDS.

"As he progressed in his narrative," says his wife, "the neighbors would come to the house from time to time to hear portions of it read, and a great interest in the work was excited among them. It claimed to have been written by one of a lost nation, and to have been recovered from the earth."

"How do you progress in deciphering the lost manuscript?" his friends used to ask.

"Come to-night to my house, and I will read you a further *translation*," the disabled clergyman would reply.

From New Salem, Ohio, Mr. Spaulding removed to Pittsburg, Pennsylvania. He there made the acquaintance of Mr. Patterson, a local editor, and showed him "The Manuscript Found," or "Book of Mormon," and lent it to him to read.

Sidney Rigdon, a cunning, vulgar man, ambitious for notoriety, and altogether low and unscrupulous, as his own correspondence shows, was connected with Mr. Patterson's printing office, and read the romance of Mr. Spaulding, made himself familiar with it, and is supposed to have copied it or large portions of it. To him the vivid tale suggested the whole imposture now known as Mormonism.

What was this romance?

It was a work in style not unlike " The Prince of the House of David " or " The Pillar of Fire." It pretended to present the primitive history of America. A colony came to the Western World from the Tower of Babel. The people were a bloody race, and became divided, and destroyed each other in a great and marvellous battle. A new colony of Jews followed them, 600 B.C. Among these were Lehi and his wife, and his sons Laman, Lemuel, Nephi, and *Sam*. (Is Uncle Sam descended from him?) They were the progenitors of the American Indians. Christ appeared to this people and preached to them forty days. A great church was founded; but after a time faith declined, and God commissioned a prophet named Mormon to write the history of this people and to hide it in the earth where it should be found in the last days.

RELICS FROM MOUNDS.

This was the romance that in an evil hour the printer Sidney Rigdon thought to be so well adapted to deceive the ignorant, and make him a leader among men, that he mastered its contents and began to preach a new revelation.

In 1805 there was born in Sharon, Vermont, a new Mahomet, who was named Joseph Smith. When he was ten years of age his parents removed to Palmyra in the State of New York, and subsequently to Manchester in the same State. The reputation of the family was bad.

We are told that the Smiths were intemperate, untruthful, addicted to stealing, and that they were shunned by honest people.

The boy was a visionary, and early turned his attention to what is dreamy and poetic in religion, without as much care about the fundamental principles of upright conduct and moral obligation. He used to retire to secret places for meditation, and here he believed that the angels began to visit him. He had a revelation, as he thought, that the end of the world was at hand.

Thus Smith grew up more bent on his visions than industry, and it only needed that he should meet Sidney Rigdon for the development of a most marvellous religious imposture.

Strangely enough, the two men met and became intimate,—Smith, with his visions still glowing in memory, and Rigdon, with poor Solomon Spaulding's Book of Mormon clearly fixed in mind.

PRETENDED FINDING OF THE PLATES.

In September, 1827, Joseph Smith pretended to have found a new

Bible. An angel, he declared, had appeared to him, and told him where the sacred record was deposited, "on the west side of a hill, not far from the top, about four miles from Palmyra."

Smith described the new revelation as engraven on plates nearly eight inches long by seven wide, a little thinner than ordinary tin, and bound together by three rings. It was written in an unknown language which he called Reformed Egyptian.

With this Bible Smith claimed to have found a pair of magic spectacles which enabled him to translate the hieroglyphics into English. These magic spectacles he called the Urim and Thummin.

But although the magic spectacles enabled him to translate "Reformed Egyptian" so admirably, they did not help him in the spelling of English words. The common school had occupied but little of Smith's time in his youthful days of visions, and he called to his assistance in writing out the new Bible in English one Oliver Cowdery, who seems to have made good use of his early opportunities at school.

The production of the new work was at once curious and commonplace. Smith would not allow the new revelation — the " Golden Bible " — to be seen by profane eyes. He hung a blanket across the middle of his room, and behind this he put on his magic spectacles and translated aloud the Reformed Egyptian, or wrote it down on slips of paper; while Oliver Cowdery, who could not read Egyptian, but could spell, sat on the other side of the blanket and put the translation into passable English text as Smith delivered it to him.

Strangely enough, the translation thus delivered proved to be the romance — " The Manuscript Found " — of poor Solomon Spaulding.

The plates on which the Bible was written mysteriously disappeared, after being shown to certain persons called " witnesses."

The revelation that Oliver Cowdery had written out from the oracle behind the blanket was printed; Joseph Smith and Sidney Rigdon began to proclaim the new doctrines of the romantic and wonderful book; the credulous flocked to hear the strange story;

converts were made; societies were formed; and the imposture grew, and became a civil and political power.

TRANSLATING THE BIBLE.

Smith preached the millennium close at hand. The Indians were to become converted, and the New Jerusalem was to arise in the very heart of America.

Whether Joseph Smith believed what he preached, or any part of

BRIGHAM YOUNG AT THE GREAT SALT LAKE

it; whether his head was turned by his supposed visions, or he was deceived by Sidney Rigdon; or whether he was conscious that he was wholly an impostor, cannot be known. This is certain; he *must* have known that the story of his magic spectacles, and his translation of the Egyptian plates behind the blanket, was a fraud.

THE END.

Rigdon, and not Smith, was the real founder of the delusion. It was he who proclaimed the strange doctrine of spiritual wives that led to polygamy.

The Mormons were driven from New York by force; they established themselves in Ohio. Their eyes turned Westward; they began to seek a land beyond the so-called Gentile world. They went to Missouri, but were expelled; they settled in Illinois, but were compelled to remove. At last they resolved to emigrate beyond civilization, and chose Utah as the territory wherein to establish the "New Jerusalem" in fulfilment of the poetic prophecies of the Golden Bible.

Joseph Smith was shot by a mob at Carthage, Illinois, in 1844. His birth and death have not the surroundings of a prophet, and the manner in which he received and imparted his revelation bear little resemblance to the lofty inspirations and stupendous events recorded in the ancient Scriptures.

To continue this strange story: —

The relatives and friends of Solomon Spaulding were astonished and grieved at the unexpected use of the old romance, " The Manuscript Found."

In 1839 his wife said in a public letter: —

After the " Book of Mormon " came out a copy of it was taken to New Salem, the place of Mr. Spaulding's former residence, and the very place where " The Manuscript Found" was written. A woman preacher appointed a meeting there, and at the meeting read and repeated copious extracts from the " Book of Mormon." The historical part was immediately recognized by all the older inhabitants as the identical work of Mr. Spaulding, in which they had been so deeply interested years before. Mr. John Spaulding was present and recognized perfectly the work of his brother. He was amazed and afflicted that it should have been perverted to so wicked a purpose. His grief found vent in tears, and he arose on the spot and expressed to the meeting his sorrow and regret that the writings of his deceased brother should be used for a purpose so vile and shocking. I am sure that nothing would grieve my husband more, were he living, than the use which has been made of his work. Thus, an historic romance, with the addition of a few pious expressions and extracts from the Sacred Scriptures, has been construed into a new Bible and palmed off upon a company of poor deluded fanatics as divine.

Sidney Rigdon, in whose evil mind and heart the imposture originated, aspired to succeed Joseph Smith as prophet and leader of the Church of the Wilderness. But the Mormon elders had learned what an insincere man Rigdon was and expelled him from the church for lying. Smith was succeeded by Brigham Young.

Salt Lake City, the so-called City of the Saints, is the historic wonder of these middle Territories. Whatever the traveller may have read about it, his eyes behold the reality with astonishment. The

MORMON TEMPLE.

grandeur of the mountain walls, the grave expanse of the great inland sea, the elegance of the public buildings, and stately and almost defiant proportions of the new Mormon Temple, combine to make the scene one to be spoken of in adjectives and interjections. It was founded in 1847 by Brigham Young and one hundred and forty-two Mormon pioneers.

It is a roomy city; most of the blocks are squares of ten acres each. The streets are eight rods wide, and the side-walks twenty feet. Most of the houses are twenty feet from the street.

"The Mormons seem to have discovered what other emigrants have failed to comprehend," said Gentleman Jo, "that there is plenty of space in the West, and that there is no reason why a city here should be built after the patterns of the Old World."

The city lies about four thousand three hundred and fifty feet above sea level. Streams of water flow down the streets under the shade trees. It contains more than twenty thousand inhabitants.

The hotels, especially the Walker House and Continental Hotel, are remarkably good; and the Class found the long piazza of the Continental Hotel a most agreeable resting-place after the long journey through Wyoming and Idaho.

The first visit made by the Class was to the new Mormon Temple, which, like the city itself, will soon be one of the wonders of the wilderness. The building is about two hundred feet long, and the foundation walls are said to be sixteen feet deep. The baptistry will be fifty-seven by thirty-seven, and the towers about two hundred feet high.

Near the Temple is the old Mormon Tabernacle, an odd looking structure which will hold thirteen thousand people. It was built in 1868, and contains one million five hundred thousand feet of lumber. Its organ has three thousand pipes. There are several Protestant churches in the city.

The Great Salt Lake, the American Dead Sea, is one of the

natural wonders of the West. It is nearly eighty miles long and forty wide. It is only about sixteen feet deep. It is a dead lake and contains nine dead islands, one of which is sixteen miles long.

The Class left Salt Lake City for Nevada and the Pacific.

Gentleman Jo interested the boys during the long and monotonous journey by descriptions of the regions through which they were passing. His conversation with them was much like illustrated history or geography lessons. In the most interesting situations his talks were like lectures. One of these palace car lectures was on

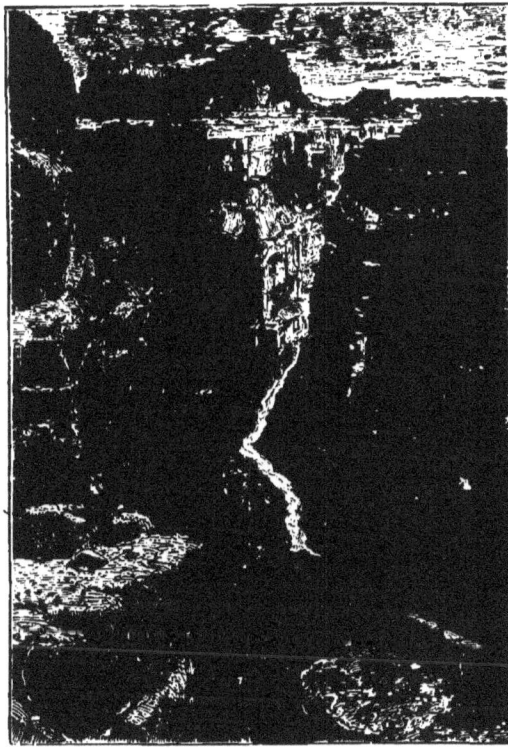

GRAND CAÑON, LOOKING EAST.

CAÑON LAND.

The Colorado River is one of the most wonderful water-courses in the world; perhaps no other river is the source of such majestic and awe-inspiring scenery.

Look upon the map of the Southwest. See the Green River draining the mountain ranges of Wyoming and Utah, and the Grand River carrying away the melting snows of the Rocky Mountains in Colorado. The two rivers unite in Utah and form the Colorado River, which forces its way through the lofty mountains of Arizona, and which for thousands of years has been tunnelling those dark and stupendous caverns known as the Grand Cañon of the Colorado.

The Colorado River is the great drain of the Rocky Mountains. It has its sources in peaks covered with everlasting snow, in lakes no eye has seen, in streams in high mountain solitudes, in regions where the clouds and waters meet, and that the human eye only looks upon from far distances. It empties the melting snows of the Rocky Mountains into the Gulf of California.

Through the long winters the snow piles itself upon the mountains. Summer comes, and the snows melt and roll and tumble down the mountain sides in millions of streams. Each of these millions of streams has its little or great cascades. Millions of tiny cascade brooks unite in thousands of creeks; the thousands of creeks form hundreds of rivulets; the rivulets become the Grand and Green Rivers, and these the mighty Colorado breaking through the mountain walls on its way to the Pacific.

Every stream, as it gathers force from the mountains, cuts deeper and deeper into the gorges, and the great rivers shatter the mountain walls and leave towering cliffs above them. These deep water-courses in broken mountains are called cañons.

Every brook runs in a cañon. The rivers form great cañons. One of the cañons of the Colorado is more than two hundred miles in length.

MARBLE CAÑON.

Cañon land is like a fable of Homer; it seems like a habitation of gods and giants. Everything is strange, wild, and weird.

The dark solitude is filled with the sound of waterfalls. A traveller might wander along the dark cliffs for days in sight of flowing streams and not be able to find a drop of water to drink.

IN THE GRAND CAÑON.

Until 1869 this marvellous region, this vast museum of natural wonders, was unknown to the world. It was then explored by Major J. W. Powell, whose narrative in his reports reads like fiction, like a tale of Homer or Virgil, like the voyages of Ulysses, or Jason's search for the Golden Fleece.

Let me relate to you some stories and incidents of Major Powell's expedition: —

A JOURNEY TO SHADOW LAND.

Major Powell started on his expedition to explore the cañons of the Colorado from Green River City, Wyoming, on May 24, 1869. His party consisted of nine men, and his outfit of four boats, with equipments for camping, with arms for defence and with provisions.

During the first few days they had no serious mishap, — they lost an oar, broke a barometer tube, and occasionally struck a bar. All around them abounded examples of that natural architecture which is seen from the passing train at the "City," — weird statuary, caverns, pinnacles, and cliffs, dyed gray and buff, red and brown, blue and black, all drawn in horizontal strata like the lines of a painter's brush. Mooring the boats and ascending the cliffs after making camp, they saw the sun go down over a vast landscape of glittering rock. The shadows fell in the valleys and gulches, and at this hour the lights became higher and the depths deeper. The Vintah Mountains stretched out in the south, thrusting their peaks into the sky, and shining as if ensheathed with silver. The distant pine forests had the bluish impenetrability of a clear night sky, and pink clouds floated in motionless suspense until, with a final burst of splendor, the light expired.

At the end of sixty-two miles they reached the mouth of Flaming Gorge, near which some hunters and Indians are settled. Flaming Gorge is a cañon bounded by perpendicular bluffs, banded with red and yellow to a height of fifteen hundred feet, and the water flowing through it is positive malachite in color, crossed and edged with glistening bars of white sand. It leads into Red Cañon, and in 1869 it was the gateway to a region which was almost wholly unknown.

An old Indian endeavored to deter Major Powell from his purpose. He held his hands high above his head, with his arms vertical, and, looking between them to the sky, said, " Rocks h-e-a-p, h-e-a-p high ; the water go h-oo-woogh, water-pony (boat) heap buck. Water catch 'em, no see 'em squaw any more, no see 'em Injin any more, no see 'em pappoose any more."

This probably was not encouraging, and with some anxiety the explorers left the last vestige of civilization behind them.

Below Flaming Gorge (so called from the brilliant color of the rocks) the explorers ran through Horseshoe Cañon, which describes an elongated letter U in the mountains, and several portages became necessary. The cliffs increased a thousand feet in height, and in many places the water completely filled the channel between them; but occasionally the cañon opened into a little park,

CLIMBING THE GRAND CAÑON.

from the grassy carpet of which sprang crimson flowers on the stems of pear-shaped cactus-plants, patches of blue and yellow blossoms, and a fragrant spiræa.

On June 1 they had an exciting ride. The river rolled down the cañon at a wonderful rate, and, with no rocks in the way, they went as fast as a train. Here and there the water rushed into a narrow gorge, and the rocks at the side rolled it into the centre in great waves, and the boats went leaping and bounding over these like things of life. They were like herds of startled deer bounding through forests beset with fallen timber. At times the waves broke over them and obliged the men to stop to bail them; once they ran twelve miles in an hour, stoppages included.

On the night of the 8th of June, as Major Powell lay awake, he saw a bright star that appeared to rest on the verge of the cliff overhead to the east. Slowly it seemed to float from its resting-place on the rock over the cañon. At first it appeared like a jewel set on the brink of the cliff; as it moved out from the rock he wondered that it did not fall. In fact, it did seem to descend in a gentle curve, as though the bright sky in which the stars were set was spread across the cañon, resting on either wall, and swayed down by its own weight. The stars appeared to be in the cañon. It was the bright star Vega, and so Major Powell called this part of the wall the Cliff of the Harp.

GRAND CAÑON OF THE COLORADO.

Day after day, wherever the men looked, there were rocks, deep gorges in which the views were lost under cliffs, towers and pinnacles, thousands of strangely carved forms, and mountains blending with the clouds.

The scenery was of unending interest. The rocks were of many colors, white, gray, pink, and purple, with saffron tints. Farther on the cliffs are of softly tinted marble, lustrously polished by the waves. At one place Major Powell walked for more than a mile on a marble pavement fretted with strange devices and embossed with a thousand different patterns. Through a cleft in the wall the sun shone on this floor, which gleamed with iridescent beauty.

Heavy clouds rolled at times in the cañon, filling it

INDIGENOUS TO THE SOIL.

with gloom. Sometimes they hung above from wall to wall, and formed a roof; then a gust of wind from a side cañon made a rift in them, and the blue heavens were revealed; or they dispersed in patches which settled on the crags, while puffs of vapor issued out of the smaller gulches, and occasionally formed bars across the cañon, one above another, each opening a different vista.

When they discharged their rains little rills first trickled down the cliff, and these soon became brooks; the brooks grew into creeks and tumbled down through innumerable cascades, which added their music to the roar of the river. As soon as the rain ceased, rills, brooks, creeks, and cascades disappeared.

On July 18 they spent the day in taking account of their damaged stores. Their flour had been wet and dried so many times that it was musty and lumpy; and though they had left Green River City with supplies for ten months, only enough for two months remained.

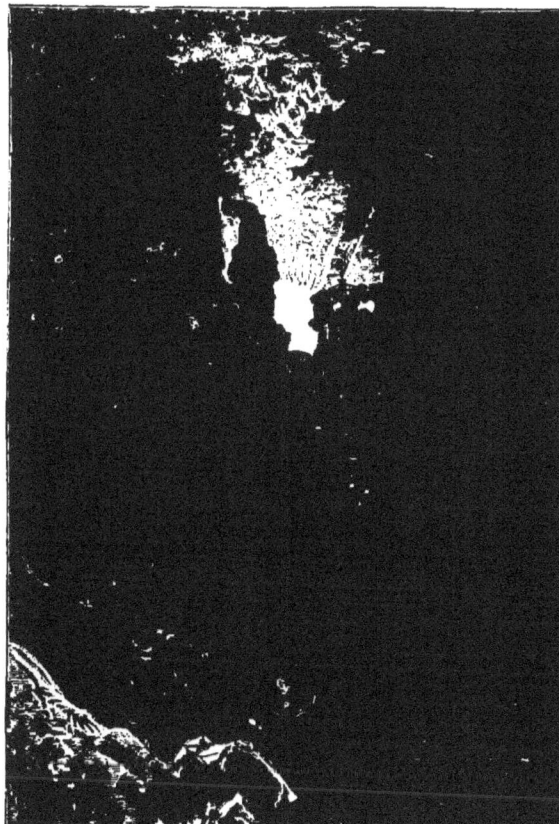

MU-KOORI-TU-WEAP CAÑON.

While in this camp they also repaired their barometer, and recalked and pitched their boats.

Major Powell and Mr. Bradley started next morning to climb the left wall below the junction of two cañons. The way they selected was up a gulch, and after climbing for an hour over and among the rocks they found themselves in a vast amphitheatre, and their way cut off. They clambered round to the left for half an hour, until they saw that they could not go up in that direction. They then tried the rocks along to the right, and discovered a narrow shelf, nearly half a mile long. In some places this was so wide that they passed along with ease; in others it was so narrow and sloping that they were compelled to lie down and crawl.

They could look over the ledge of the shelf, down eight hundred feet, and see the river rolling and plunging among the rocks. Looking up five hundred feet to the brink of the cliff, it seemed to blend with the sky.

They continued along until they came to a point where the wall was again broken down. On the right there was a narrow, mural point of rock, extending towards the river, two or three hundred feet high, and six or eight hundred feet long. They came back to where this set in, and found it cut off from the main wall by a great crevice. Into this they passed, and down a long narrow rock which was between them and the river. This rock itself was split and full of crevices. The crevices were usually narrow above, and, by erosion of the streams flowing over them from the plateau, wider below, forming a network of caves, each cave having a narrow winding sky-light.

They wandered along these for an hour or two, but saw no place where they could climb up. At

AT THE FOOT OF THE GRAY CAÑON.

last they attempted a passage by a crevice which they thought was wide enough to admit their bodies, and yet narrow enough to allow them to climb out by pressing their hands and feet against the walls. So they climbed as men would climb out of a well. Bradley went first, and the major handed him the barometer, and then climbed over his head. Afterwards the major took the barometer from Bradley, and the latter climbed over the major.

So they passed each other alternately, until they emerged from the fissure out on the summit of the rock.

What a world of grandeur was then spread before them! Below was the cañon, through which the Colorado runs. They could trace its course for miles, and at points catch glimpses of the river. From the northwest came the Green in a narrow, winding gorge. From the northeast came the Grand, through a cañon that seemed bottomless from where they stood.

Away to the west were lines of cliffs and ledges of rock,—not such ledges as you may have seen where the quarryman splits his blocks, but ledges from which the gods might quarry mountains, that, rolled out on the plain below, would stand a lofty range; and not such cliffs as you may have seen where the swallow builds its nest, but cliffs where the eagle is lost to view before he reaches the summit.

Between them and the distant cliffs were the strangely carved and pinnacled rocks of the Toom-piu wro-near Tu weap. On the summit of the opposite wall of the cañon were more strange rock-forms. Away to the east a group of eruptive mountains was seen, the Sierra La Sal. Their slopes were covered with pines, and the deep gulches were flanked with great crags and snow-fields near the summits. The mountains were in uniform, green, gray, and silver.

ISLAND MONUMENT.

Thus down into shadow land, on the "water-ponies," over a highway of continuous rapids the bold explorers went on, and returned at last like Æneas from the lower world, to relate, unlike Æneas, a narrative of facts that read like fable.

Nevada: another unsettled empire, vast, rich, grand. More than one hundred and twelve thousand square miles, more than seventy-

ON THE COLORADO RIVER.

one million acres. An almost limitless plain walled by mountains that are covered mines of silver and gold, — great banks. as it were, to supply the money marts of the world. It is a land of the sage-brush and scanty water supply; of a Pacific summer and an Atlantic winter; of mountain walls green at the base and white at the summits; of immense distances from the sage-brush valleys to the heights of eternal snow.

Here are the richest silver mines in the world. Here come men famishing for gold; here they are fed, depart, and die. Here men glitter like Solomon, and, like him, sum up the experience of life at last in the confession, — " all is vanity."

The cars swept on over the wide, vast plains towards the city of the Golden Gate, — the Ophir of the Occident.

CHAPTER XIII.

SAN FRANCISCO.

THE WONDERFUL HOTEL. — THE CHINESE QUESTION. — THE BIG TREES. — STORY OF
"LORD WHEELBARROW" AND THE "WRATTLE-SNAKE." — THE YOSEMITE.

HE Class entered San Francisco in the evening. The boys were very tired, and went immediately to their rooms at the hotel after a late supper.

"What means all this magnificence?" asked Charlie Leland of Gentleman Jo in the morning. "I should think we were in a royal residence. Where are we?"

"In the finest palace hotel in the world."

"Away out here in the West?"

"Yes."

Gentleman Jo and Charlie went out for a walk. To Charlie the streets seemed like a bazaar of all nations.

They paused before the new City Hall, a colossal structure of art swallowing up millions of gold, as though the land were indeed an Ophir and the city fathers in reality Solomons.

They went to Telegraph Hill, and there took their first views of the Pacific. San Francisco Bay glimmered in the sunlight. Beyond the bay were the mountains terminating with the conical peak of Mount Diablo.

Below was the city of the Golden Land, and beside it the ships and steamships of all nations lay like a city of the sea. Over the blue harbor floated the flags of China, Japan, Australia, and all the nations that border on the Pacific.

"In 1847," said Gentleman Jo, "San Francisco was nothing but a town. Two Catholic missionaries of the order of St. Francis estab-

PALACE HOTEL AT SAN FRANCISCO.

lished a mission here in 1776, and called it the Mission Dolores. A town sprung up around the mission and it received the name Yerba Buena, or 'good herb,' from a plant that grew here and was used for tea.

"Gold! I well remember the cry, the excitement, the surprising emigration. The new Territory on the Pacific was a land of gold!

IN ASIA.

How men left their families! How they doubled Cape Horn! How they perished on the sands of Panama!

"Yerba Buena became San Francisco. In 1848 its population was one thousand; in 1850 it was twenty-five thousand; it more than doubled during the next ten years, and this immense increase was nearly trebled in the next decade.

"Here is the city to-day. What a wonder! She sits distributing gold to all nations, and ranks with the queen cities of Asia that ferry the Pacific from the marts of trade that have flourished for thousands of years."

Whenever the Class returned from a walk, the Palace Hotel called forth from the boys some expression of admiration.

"It is like a hotel built for all the world," said Charlie.

"And you may find in it representatives from every nation," said Gentleman Jo.

"How much ground does it cover?" asked Tommy, on seeing its roofs from an elevated part of the city.

"Nearly two and a quarter acres," answered Gentleman Jo.

"Such an hotel ought not to be here," said Tommy.

"Where ought it to be?" asked Gentleman Jo.

"In *Boston!*"

"Oh! But, as you have seen from your journey, a considerable part of the world lies outside of Boston."

"So I perceive," said Tommy, just then getting a first view of the Chinese quarter. "I am glad that this part of the world does lie outside of Boston."

"Here we are," said Gentleman Jo.

"Where?" asked Tommy.

"In Asia."

The street seemed full of old curiosity shops, piled one upon another, high in air. The Chinese inhabitants looked inoffensive enough, and the boys were surprised to hear a San Francisco officer who accompanied Master Lewis say, —

"They are the curse of our city, — a heathen and a Christian race cannot exist side by side."

"I should think that Christian churches would establish missions among them," said Tommy.

"Just as well establish missions in a town of prairie dogs," said the public officer.

The remark seemed to excite the indignation of Gentleman Jo.

"You may think so," he said, "but the Chinese nation had advanced a thousand years in civilization when your ancestors and mine were barbarians wandering about in sheepskins."

"What did they ever accomplish?"

"Discovered the mariner's compass."

"What has that to do with America?"

"America was discovered by the means of it."

"Oh!"

"Yes."

"What else did the Chinese ever do?"

"Invented the art of printing."

"That may all be true," said the officer, "but if you were a teacher in San Francisco, and had two thousand dollars' salary, and one of these wise Celestial people should apply for your place, and offer to teach for one half that salary, you would not like it. That is the way laboring men feel."

"While our country needs laborers, would it not be well to meet the Chinese in the Christian spirit," said Gentleman Jo, "and to aim to do as much for their moral development as they do for the development of the physical resources of the country? I have not studied this question very closely, but I believe on broad general principles that a man is a man, and the rights of men are equal. There are common principles that apply to all races, and the best of these is,— 'Whatsoever ye would that men should do to you, do ye even so to them.' Believing this, I have no sympathy with the politics or

GIANT TREES OF CALIFORNIA.

Christianity represented by some of your public men. Still, I may be wrong, and our civilization may be in danger of corruption by these new people. Time will tell."

The Class went to Stockton, and there secured ponies and pack mules for a journey to the Yosemite.

It was a four days' ride, and proved a tiresome journey. The occasional sight of a Digger Indian, prairie dog, or a horned lizard, relieved the monotony. Once the party met a miner from the East; he had

A SECTION.

had Jerry Slack's inspiration, but it had been followed by bad luck, and the money-pot at the foot of the Western rainbow had not been found, although he had dug for it.

In the afternoon of the fourth day the Class came in sight of the "big trees."

"The spires of Nature's cathedral," said Wyllys.

"Yaas," said the guide, "Joe Rollins diskivered um in '52. When he told folks about um nobody believed him, and no wonder. That there old feller yonder is more than two hundred feet high, and about fifty feet round. Joe never told a lie, Joe did n't."

The Class had never heard of this pioneer who possessed such Washingtonian virtues.

"Here we come to one," said the guide, "that you can ride through on a mule, right through the trunk as it lies there capsized, and you 'll come out sixty feet further down. That tree must have held its head high in its day, — sort of a king of trees it must have been; just enter through that there knot-hole. I know of one tree so large that you can ride through its trunk in a wagon."

BIG TREE TUNNEL.

The so-called "big trees" are some two hundred in number and occupy a tract of land about two miles square. Some of them may be a thousand years old. The circumference of one of them was more than ninety feet, and several of them were more than three hundred feet high.

"You come from Bosting?" said the guide.

"Yes," said Charlie, with the emphasis of local pride.

"Tell ye what, I 've been told that ye could put Bunker Hill Monument right inside of one of them 'ere trees, and have considerable space left beside. How is it?"

"Bunker Hill Monument," said Gentleman Jo, "is two hundred

EXHAUSTING THE POISON.

and twenty feet high. As some of these trees are three hundred and twenty feet in height, the monument could be hidden in one of them, with a hundred feet of tree-top above it."

On the journey the Class not only met with Digger Indians, Chinese miners, and seedy adventurers, but some very curious specimens of natural history. Among the latter were the repulsive

PRAIRIE DOGS.

horned lizard, and some cunning prairie dogs and their social-looking habitations.

Here, among the prairie dogs, by a mere accident, the boys saw the first rattlesnake in all their journey from the Atlantic to the Pacific. Tommy asked the guide to kill the snake that he might have the rattles for a "trophy." The guide attacked the snake quite fearlessly, which caused surprise.

"I would ha' caught him for you alive, if you had asked me," said the guide, delivering to Tommy the dead snake.

"Alive!" said Tommy, shrinking suspiciously from the dead reptile. "How?"

"How? The way the Indians do. Just put a piece of meat on to the end of a stick, and hold it out to the snake and let him bite at it, till he exhausts his poison. Then he is as harmless as a rabbit. Take him right up with your hands. Mebbe I 'll diskiver another; if I do I 'll get him for you."

"For *me!*" said Tommy, looking nervous, "I would n't touch one for a thousand dollars, no, not for all the gold in California."

"You make me think of Lord Wheelbarrer," said the guide.

"Lord who?"

"Wheelbarrer," answered the guide. "It seems to me that was the name; it sounded like it, but did not look quite that way when it was all spelled out."

"LORD WHEELBARROW" AND THE "WRATTLESNAKE."

There wer' a lot of those great English gentry used to wander over the West naturalizin'. There was Lord Dunraven, — he was the "Great Divide" man; kind o' struck on the Yellowstone Park; wrote a book about it; I 'spose you read it. Then there was *Sir* this one, *Sir* that one, and last of all who should come out here to see the big trees and the Yosemite but Lord Wheelbarrer, as they called him! I never knew whether that was his name or not; it did not sound quite so flowin' and flowery as Dunraven.

I conducted a large party from Stockton to the Yosemite by the way of Mariposa. They were great on bugs and bears, and all kinds of creeping things, that party was, and none of um used such blown-out words as Lord Wheelbarrer. When he first saw a Digger Indian he acted as though he had met with a long-lost brother.

Well, on the way he came across a snake, a whopper. He called it a "wrattlesnake," — he kind of wabbled his words, left off the *h's* where they belonged and put um on to words where they did n't belong. Why, he would call a mountain an *helevation*.

Lord Wheelbarrer asked me to capture the snake alive, and I put a piece of meat on the end of a pole, and was about to draw the poison, when I dis-

THE YOSEMITE VALLEY.

covered that it was not a rattlesnake. I said nothing, but just held it in a fixed place by the pole and seized it by the tail, and brought it to Lord Wheelbarrer. He was the scaredest man I ever saw.

"A wrattle, wrattle—" said he, gasping, and while he was wabblin away, the snake slipped out of my hand, and flopped over into the Lord's big boot.

You should have just heard that Hinglishman yell. I pulled the snake away, and then that man, what did he do but wilted right away.

"The poison has taken effect," said he, "and I am a dyin'. Send these things to Ann Hoxey," said he.

"Ann Hoxey?" said I. "Who's she?"

"My wife."

"Lady Wheelbarrer?"

THE LONG LOST BROTHER.

"Oh dear, no. I 'm not a real live lord,— or sha'n't be long."

"You 're not goin' to die," said I.

"Why not? I 'll give you all I 'm worth if you will save my life."

"That wa'n't a rattlesnake," said I.

He rose right up like a giant and never spoke a word. In a few hours we met some miners going to 'Frisco, and Lord Wheelbarrer jined um, and he never so much as lifted his hat to me to say "Thank ye" or "Good-by."

It was a bright afternoon, like September in New England. The trail led around the point of a huge rock, and suddenly the guide waved his arms, pointed downward, and said,—

"The Yosemite!"

Why attempt to describe the scene that came into view? No pen can do it. Even Bierstadt's pencil fails. To call it a rocky cavern five or eight miles long, nearly a mile broad and a mile deep, conveys no correct impression of the grandeur, vastness, and immensity of this temple of nature in which the Divine Architect reveals his wisdom, glory, and power.

The Flume in the White Mountains is a miniature Yosemite, but the tens of feet of its walls must be multiplied by hundreds and thousands to make it convey an impression of the cleft mountains of the Sierras. The mountain walls of the Franconia Notch, New Hampshire, were they separated at a distance of a mile apart, would be but a half Yosemite; divide, in your imagination, Mt. Lafayette in the middle and set its perpendicular walls on either side of a green valley, and you may see the Yosemite.

The Class passed "El Capitan," which is an immense granite cliff, three thousand three hundred feet high, the most stupendous rock monument of its kind in the world; the Bridal Veil Falls, with its feathery foam, seeming like a crystal ladder reaching to heaven; the Cathedral Spires, which are needles of rock, rising above the valley two thousand six hundred feet; spires such as no cathedral built with human hands ever had. What are the two hundred and twenty feet of Bunker Hill Monument in comparison with these?

Near the end of this seven-mile journey, through this street of a rock city whose towers touched the sky, the Class rested in view of the Nevada Fall. Here the river leaps into the valley from a height of seven hundred feet.

Look up. Mountains rise over mountains. Measurements fail. Metaphors fail. It is God's church, Nature's cathedral, and to it the temples of man are like toys.

NEVADA FALL

CHAPTER XIV.

ANCIENT AMERICA.

ZUÑIS. — PUEBLO INDIANS. — LEADVILLE. — COLORADO. — GARDEN OF THE GODS.

WE are now on our way to ancient America," said Gentleman Jo.
The Class was entering Arizona by rail on the way to Santa Fé, New Mexico.
"When the Spanish discoverers beheld the palaces of Mexico glittering with gold," said Gentleman Jo, "they asked Montezuma where he obtained this wealth.
"'From the Northwest,' answered the king.
"The Spaniards ascertained that the treasure country of the golden city of Mexico was Cibola. Cortez sent twenty trustworthy men to find Cibola. The men never returned.
" We are now entering the old kingdom of Cibola, a part of America that was explored nearly one hundred years before the Pilgrims landed at Plymouth. Here came Coronado in 1540. Santa Fé is, with the exception of St. Augustine, Florida, the oldest town in the United States. Many think it may claim to be older than St. Augustine.
"'The wealth of the world will be found in New Mexico and Ari-

zona,' said Humboldt. These Territories are not only famous for their mines, and the beauty and grandeur of their natural scenery, but for the descendants of very ancient and mysterious races that inhabit them. Some historians believe that these original inhabitants first came from Egypt, by the way of Behring's Straits; that they are the descendants of the nations of the expelled Shepherd Kings. Others think them to have been the lost ten tribes of Israel; and still others emigrants from the great island of Atlantis, believed to have sunk in the sea."

THE ZUNIS.

Colonel A. W. Doniphan, who commanded the first American expedition that marched through the Territory of New Mexico, in the year 1846, called attention to the fact that there was living in that Territory a race of Pueblo, or town, Indians. These Indians claimed to be directly descended from the famous Aztec race, who inhabited Mexico at the time the Conquerors took possession of it in 1521.

The colonel stated still further, that this people worshipped the sun, and inherited and followed many of the traditions and customs as described by the historians of the Cortez expedition.

A few years ago, said Gentleman Jo, I determined to visit these descendants of a people, who, years before Columbus discovered America, were living in comfortable dwellings constructed of stone, six stories in height, — a people who manufactured not only their own clothing, ornaments, and household utensils, but cultivated the soil most successfully, and the ruins of whose wonderful towns are now known to cover a section of country hundreds of miles in extent.

At the time of my visit none of the pueblos lying east of the Rio Bravo del Norte were inhabited, the last one, Pecos, having been abandoned a year or two previous. These Indians then numbered about ten thousand souls, living in eight or ten pueblos, the principal of which were Taos, Zuñi, Jemez, Laguna, Acoma, and the seven Moqui cities.

These pueblos are built of stone, and in outward appearance resemble a large fort. There is no communication between the lower stories and the street. The only manner of gaining access to the houses is by means of ladders. These are always drawn up at night, thus effectually guarding the inhabitants against intrusion.

The buildings are generally from three to six stories in height. Each story recedes from the one below; a kind of terrace or verandah is thus formed, on which the people pass many hours daily.

Each pueblo that I visited was provided with an *estufa*, or underground apartment, which is dedicated to religious purposes. The only light or air in the room is obtained from a scuttle in the roof, which also affords the only mode of ingress and egress.

RESTORATION OF PUEBLO BONITO.

It was upon the altars in these *estufas* that the sacred fire was kept burning for so many generations.

This they claim to have done in obedience to a command from Montezuma, who assured them that if they preserved the sacred fire and did not permit the eyes of their conquerors to behold it, he would one day return, bringing with him men from the East, when he would conduct his children away from the land inhabited by their conquerors, the Spaniards.

At the time I visited these pueblos, it was no uncommon thing to see these Indians upon a fine morning sitting upon the roofs of their houses, their faces turned towards the East, anxiously watching for the first appearance of the god of day, upon whose fiery chariot-wheels Montezuma was expected to return for the purpose of leading his people to their promised land.

The implicit faith that these poor Indians have in the ultimate return of Montezuma is in itself sublime. So perfect is it that neither the lapse of centuries, nor the threats or persuasions of the Catholic priests who, since 1693, have been in the country, have succeeded in shaking it in the slightest degree.

ROOM IN THE MOKI HOUSE.

The pueblo of the Zuñi was doubtless one of the cities of Cibola. It was standing, old and gray, when the Spanish conquerors found it in 1538. It is in New Mexico, not far from the Arizona boundary.

Gentle, peace-loving Indians are the Zuñis, living in primitive simplicity, and devoting their lives to industry and religion, as they did when visited by Coronado, the old Spanish chieftain. They have lately made a young white man one of their chiefs.

ANCIENT AMERICA.   305

We will not add a written description of these pueblos to Gentleman Jo's narrative, but will let the artist give the reader very correct pictorial views of the habitations, manners, and customs of the Pueblo Indians.

The Spaniards established themselves in Santa Fé in 1555. It is a dreamy old place. The streets are full of idlers, who move about mechanically; many of these people are very old, for the reason that they are not active enough to wear out life's machinery. The old "Adobe Palace" and the Guadalupe Church remind one of the days

THE RAILROAD CREPT TO THE REGIONS OF THE SUN.

of the Jesuits and of the glory of Spain, long faded. The Palace Hotel, erected at a cost of one hundred thousand dollars, rises over the low houses and speaks of the era of progress close at hand.

One day's walks revealed all of interest that was to be seen in Santa Fé, and the Class was next swept along the rail amid growing surprises of natural scenery to "Pueblo."

Colorado, called the Centennial State because admitted to the

20

RESTORATION OF PUEBLO HUNJO PAVIE.

Union in 1876, is apparently about to become a famous industrial region of rolling mills and machine shops, smelters and blast furnaces, oil wells and refineries, — the Pennsylvania of the West, a region of mighty energies and activities, an empire that will uprear a monumental history. Here the lost cities of Cibola are to rise again. As Minnesota is the New England of the Northwest, so is Colorado the New England of the Southwest.

Pueblo is a wonder. It commands the trade of the mountain mines. It pulses with activity and seems to grow in the night.

And now the white head of Pike's Peak, and of other mountains almost as high, began to glow sharp and clear in the sky. Along the backbone of the continent the branch of the Denver and Rio Grande Railroad crept "to the regions of the sun," Tommy said, "letting the world go." On no other railroad in the world are such awe-inspiring scenes to be witnessed. The

ZUNIS

world did indeed seem lost, and everything to disclose majesty, power, and glory, around, above, beneath.

"Yesterday we left the oldest city in the United States; to-morrow we shall visit the youngest," said Gentleman Jo, on the rail, amid the surprises of peaks and cañons, gloomy solitudes, and garish light.

LEADVILLE.

Every one hears of Leadville, the city that has arisen out of the wilderness in so short a time, — the great carbonate camp in which some men have made themselves millionnaires, while others have toiled on in the rugged mountain sides, hoping that each stroke of the pick would reveal to them a mineral belt in which all fortunes are found.

A few years ago there was no Leadville, and to-night one may look down on crowded streets full of all the activity that is not known in the larger Eastern cities.

The city is situated at an altitude of ten thousand three hundred feet above sea level, and on the western side of Bald Mountain. On the east, towering grandly, the snow-crowned peaks of the Musquito Range lift their heads high up above us, while on the south and west is the Main, or Snowy Range, that separates the rivers of the continent; this range is sometimes called the "Backbone of the Continent."

This region was the scene of the great gold excitement in 1859 and 1860. It is estimated that twenty thousand persons were here then, and placer mining was carried on to a very large extent. Several millions of dollars in gold were secured, and then the supply became exhausted, and the seekers of wealth sought more promising fields, not knowing of the rich treasures just below their feet; and it was not until the fall of 1877 that the value of hard and soft carbonates became understood through what is roughly termed a "grub stake," the meaning of which title I will explain.

When some of the miners become so poor that they are not able to furnish the necessary tools and "grub" with which to "go prospecting," a third party of sufficient means offers to furnish tools and provisions on condition that he be given a certain interest in anything that may be found.

In the spring of 1878 two miners secured a "grub stake" from a pioneer, who is now an ex-Governor, but was at that time the proprietor of a small grocery store in the little village of Oro. The discovery of the famous "Little

Pittsburg" mine was the result of the "grub stake" referred to, and the two miners became independent, while the small capitalist is one of the richest men in the State, and the net profit of the mine has paid to its owners more than one million dollars.

Then came from the east and the west, from the north and the south, multitudes of eager, expectant men, ready to give up their comfortable homes and endure the privations of a new mining camp in the midst of cheerless mountains, and the wearisome toil of a "prospector," if a lucky stroke of the pick

MINING IN COLORADO.

would only reveal to them the beds of rich mineral that were now known to lie hidden in the gray and rugged mountains.

In this eager race for fortune there are no conditions of wealth and superior intelligence in favor of the lucky ones. The poorest and most ignorant man, provided with a shovel and pick, has equal chances with the man of wealth or

ROOM IN PUEBLO OF TAOS.

the learned graduate who can give in wonderful geological terms all the formations of the earth.

The precious deposits are found in so many different conditions, and there is so little similarity in different sections, that no set rule or indication can be relied on.

Sometimes ore is found within fifteen feet of the surface, and within four hundred yards of that place it may be necessary to go down three hundred feet before the "indications" are found that assure the toilers that the reward of their labor is near at hand.

The cost of producing ore does not exceed fifteen per cent of its value, and one wagon-load of the precious mineral has contained six thousand dollars in silver.

Sunday is a kind of high carnival, for then the miners come down from their dreary homes on the mountain sides to lay in their weekly store of provisions, and to make the day one of merriment in the dance and gambling halls.

Almost within sound of the congregation singing, —

"Jesus, lover of my soul,"

a thousand men sit at keno and faro tables, hearing only the "call" of the keno dealers, and closing their hearts and their ears to the more earnest voice that bids them to remember that their souls' interests are of more value than silver or gold.

It is surprising to see how regular and even the streets of Leadville are, when we remember how suddenly the city sprang up.

Harrison Avenue, State, and Chestnut are the principal streets, and it is on these thoroughfares that the greatest multitudes are seen. Broadway, New York, cannot be more thronged than Harrison Avenue just after sunset. It is a gay, merry, and motley crowd one finds there. Every face wears an animated look, and sympathetic souls are not annoyed by the sight of thinly clad and suffering beggars pleading for alms.

There are seemingly no poor people here; all have enough to eat and wear, and I have never seen a beggar on the street.

Life in Leadville tends to prodigality and the squandering of one's substance, and the people seem to have no fear of a "rainy day." In case of reverses some of them would suffer, for the average miner is a generous and gay personage, who often spends at night all he makes during the day.

A mining city is full of temptations to one who has abnormal tendencies to evil. Leadville is also a city in which weak young men can develop energy and self-reliance. But many a young man, the pride and joy of some Eastern home, lies in that most desolate and dreary of places, the Leadville cemetery ; and there are more funerals without mourners there than in any other graveyard in the West. You would not suppose that the express wagon clattering so merrily over the stones, with a whistling son of Nimshi holding the reins, was a Leadville funeral train, and yet that is often what it is.

Denver, the Queen City of the Plains, the Boston of the Southwest, the Geneva of America!

It occupies an altitude of five thousand one hundred and ninety-seven feet, twelve miles from the Rocky Mountains. It was born in 1858. In 1860 it was a place of log-cabins and tents; to-day it stands a marvel of beauty and taste, with fifty thousand inhabitants.

Manitou is the Saratoga of the West. It has an elevation of more than six thousand feet, and is shut in on three sides by Pike's Peak and its attendant sentinels.

Pike's Peak is fourteen thousand three hundred and thirty-six feet high, the Mont Blanc of America.

All that the Class had before seen became dwarfed by the stupendous spectacle that here presented itself. In this land of the sage-brush and the cactus, of gray solitudes and desolations, Nature uplifts her contrasts in prodigal beauty and colossal splendors. The tourist lives, as it were, in the air.

The hotels of Manitou were full of consumptives, — people with weak lungs and strong intellects, who had come here as to a shrine, praying Nature for life.

The recoveries from consumption are often wonderful here, but it is not safe for the convalescents to return East. They must remain in this dry air until a complete change has taken place in their constitutions and habits, and this change involves years of residence in the clear, pure air.

Says Mrs. H. H. Jackson, who came to Colorado for her health and remained there several years: —

For the benefit of persons who from sickness are under the necessity of seeking a change of climate, let me try to answer the question, what is, and what is not, to be expected from the Colorado climate.

It is not specifically curative. It is not a medicine. It can often arrest consumption, in the earlier stages of that disease, simply because the air is so dry that the lung tissues cannot go on altering. Ulcers on internal surfaces dry up, just as the external skin dries up when deprived of moisture.

Owing to this, the disease is arrested ; nature has a chance to attend to her own instinctive healing ; the patient is better ; gains strength ; feels himself saved.

Often after this result is secured the patient goes back to the East. Of course, he breaks down again in a few months with the same or with a worse trouble, and then it is said that Colorado did not do him any real good after all.

The trouble was not with Colorado, but the man and his friends had expected too much. He might have lived to a good old age in Colorado. While he was there his disease was like an enemy whose weapons were taken away, and whose hands were tied. Going back to the lower altitude and moister air, he freed his enemy and put the weapons into his hands again.

In the case of asthma, which is the only disease of which it is safe to say that it is nearly always relieved in Colorado, what I have said about a change of climate is also true.

The asthmatic patient breathes here with ease. He says, " I am well." So long as he stays in Colorado, Colorado will compel his lungs to do him good service, but she gives no guaranteed passports to asthmatics to go beyond her lines.

In the cases of more advanced consumption, there is, of course, less benefit to be expected from the climate of Colorado. Still, there are many persons living here in fairly comfortable health, able to do some work, who have very serious organic disease. They will probably die of consumption in Colorado, but it will be several years later than they would have died at the East.

Perhaps the invalids, next to the asthmatics, who are surest to be helped here in Colorado are those suffering from general debility and prostration.

There is a marvellous tonic in the dry air and in the sunshine. But to reap this benefit the weakened patients must lead out-door lives, and obey strictly all the laws of health, which in nine cases out of ten they have been in the habit of breaking at home.

The Class made an excursion from Manitou in carriages to Colorado

Springs, another colony of invalids. Here in the clear, dry, life-giving air, which the lungs drink in as fevered lips drink from a fountain, many an invalid who had lost hope has felt the glow of health coming back again. Here, too, many have found graves.

The ride from Manitou to the Garden of the Gods is perhaps the grandest that can be made on the continent. Only the journey from Geneva to Chamouni surpasses it in any of the routes of travel that are common to the tourist.

The Garden of the Gods, mighty, unreal, awe-inspiring! The valley is well named, not that it would suggest a garden of the beauty-loving gods of Greece, but a shrine of the colossal deities of the Sierras and the plateau of the Rocky Mountains. The Indians called the region Manitou — God.

Nature made the garden, and it is one of her masterpieces.

For ages the air and running water have worn the rocks into the wonderful and fantastic shapes that here confront and astonish the traveller, — monuments, towers, battlemented summits, stupendous columns, gloomy and picturesque ruins, — like Palmyra, Nineveh, Athens, had they been smitten by an earthquake in their palmy days, and their colonnades left despoiled of the finer beauties of art.

It is a solitude, such a solitude as can be found nowhere else in the world. Here are lovely velvet lawns, stately pines, grand oaks. Here the winds continually sigh, and the water murmurs in its flow. The encircling mountains oppress the mind; the clear, blue, illimitable sky over all impresses one with thoughts of the Infinite and Eternal.

Words cannot produce it. You pass between lofty portals of rock of terra cotta red, and find the garden carpeted with flowers and mosses, and strewn, as it were, with precious stones. The imagination turns the weird columns into living statues. Here is a castle in ruins; yonder a colossal eagle perched on an eminence; here a leaning tower, there a cube resting on a slender pivot as though a child might overturn it; a house balanced in air. All is scintillant with

GARDEN OF THE GODS.

color. The sky-piled masonry everywhere blazes in the sun, and the sunshine of Colorado is a golden glory, as wonderful as the crystal air.

Here our narrative ends. The Class returned from Denver by express trains to Altoona, and there stopped to enjoy the grand scenery of the Alleghanies.

From Philadelphia the Class make a detour to Baltimore, Washington, and Mount Vernon. The boys saw the Capitol at Washington by moonlight, one of the most beautiful sights in the world.

"Well, Herman," said Gentleman Jo, as the Class was approaching Boston, "what are your views now of the opportunities of young men in the West?"

"One cannot rightly judge from a two months' excursion," said Herman. "A young man can do as well in the East as in the West. Life will here open to him greater resources. He will have more helps. But too many helps do not enable some young men to develop themselves, or make them self-reliant. Going West, in the case of a young man with a right purpose, tends to good health, morals, and success. It leads to the right use of one's own resources of body, brain, and principles. It is the best thing to do if one cannot do better. I think it may be my duty to go. It might be wrong for Wyllys to do so; he seems to have better advantages for success here."

"The West gives a purpose to many lives," said Gentleman Jo. "It is full of hopes, promises, inspiration. What many lives need is inspiration, for too many of us form habits that make us like, well—"

"Poor Jerry Slack," concluded Herman.

"But Jerry Slacks are not the kind of men the great West needs," said Master Lewis. "Jerry Slacks do not build Chicagos or carry railroads over the Sierras. She wants men of decision, nerve, fibre, and character. America has only begun to fulfil her destiny. She exists only in outline.

"Our rapid journey has enabled you to glance at the possibilities of our nation. It has drawn a picture in your imagination. You have looked upon America from the mountain tops. What you have seen will make you more patriotic and better citizens. It will make you feel that you owe a duty to caucuses and election days. It will, I hope, enable you to vote more intelligently, and always for the highest principles and the best men.

"As to the question whether a young man should go West or remain in the East, I will return the same answer I made when you first discussed the subject at Yule: Let each one follow his own inspiration and sense of duty; let each one live his life."

He then again quoted Tennyson's "Audley Court:" —

>"Oh! who would fight and march and countermarch,
>Be shot for sixpence in a battle-field,
>And shovelled up into a bloody trench
>Where no one knows? But let me live my life.
>
>"Oh! who would cast and balance at a desk,
>Perched like a crow upon a three-legged stool,
>Till all his juice is dried. and all his joints
>Are full of chalk? But let me live my life.
>
>"Who 'd serve the state? For if I carved my name
>Upon the cliffs that guard my native land,
>I might as well have traced it in the sands;
>The sea wastes all: but let me live my life."

www.ingramcontent.com/pod-product-compliance
Lightning Source LLC
Chambersburg PA
CBHW022018240426
43667CB00042B/931